WELCOME TO THE WONDERFUL
WORLD OF NUMEROLOGY!

Just by knowing what a number represents and
applying that information to your birth certificate
name and birthdate, you can learn about:
- your love life
- your future
- your dreams of success
- your strengths and weaknesses
- your inner nature
- your purpose in life
- and much, much more!

Renowned numerologist Karen David makes it
fascinating—and fun—to uncover the secrets
of numbers, and see how they influence every
aspect of your health and happiness.

She's got *your* number, so read on!

I'VE GOT YOUR NUMBER

*Using Numerology's Secrets
to Shape Your Life*

Karen David

BANTAM NONFICTION ™

BANTAM BOOKS
NEW YORK • TORONTO • LONDON • SYDNEY • AUCKLAND

I'VE GOT YOUR NUMBER

A Bantam Book/published by arrangement with the author

PRINTING HISTORY

Originally published as Numerology Asks: Who Do You Think You Are Anyway?

RKM Publishing Company edition published 1982

Bantam edition/April 1992

ISBN 0-553-29668-X

Published simultaneously in the United States and Canada

Bantam Books are published by Bantam Books, a division of Bantam Doubleday Dell Publishing Group, Inc. Its trademark, consisting of the words "Bantam Books" and the portrayal of a rooster, is Registered in U.S. Patent and Trademark Office in other countries. Marca Registrada. Bantam Books, 666 Fifth Avenue, New York, New York 10103.

PRINTED IN THE UNITED STATES OF AMERICA

OPM   0 9 8 7 6 5 4 3 2 1

Dedication

Foremost, to Eileen Nauman, noted women's-fiction author, medical astrologer, and medicine woman. You are and always will be my very special friend, "sister" in my heart, and fellow traveler on the Path. Your support, encouragement, and buffer against adversity is unprecedented. Thank you for all of it. Love you.

To Joey Crinita, fellow author, metaphysician, and medium who has been a long time friend. When we first met, an invisible tie of feeling like we've known each other forever was created. Since then, you never fail to make me laugh, supply your insight, or share yourself. Time or distance has no bearing on our connection.

To my mom, Jerri, my step-dad Dave, who became like a real father, and my sister Cheryl. Even during the times of not knowing exactly where my type of calling would take me, thanks for accepting my being "unordinary."

Acknowledgments

A book is never done by just one person. It breathes a life by the backup of other sources, minds, and hearts. I'd like to thank Bantam Books, Danelle McCafferty, freelance editor, and Jim Skinner, broadcasting consultant for your belief and support; Barbara Alpert, my senior editor, for the free hand you gave to me on additions and changes; Maureen Walters, my agent, for helping make this book fly.

Thank you.

KAREN J. DAVID

Special Thanks

To Anthony M. Gentile, President, of Richard Stevens Cosmetics for spreading the "good word"; Phil Elia, Sr., for the special link you kept alive between us; George Novotney, Jr., attorney and my former husband for the help both personally and legally; Joan Todd, Gayle, Fred & Kim, Bev, and all my friends, students and clients who cared enough throughout the years . . . THANK YOU WITH ALL MY HEART!

Contents

Foreword

▲ I first met Karen back in 1978 and was immediately impressed with her keen perception of numerology and its overlap into the world of people and their problems. Having worked with her over the years, I'm convinced that numerology and astrology are sister sciences that work hand in hand with one another. Perhaps Karen's greatest contribution to astrology is contained in Chapter 12, in which she discusses the assignment of numbers to planets. Her accuracy is uncanny in this department and leaves astrologers with much food for thought. There have been instances when I've found numerology provided greater insight than astrology, and I believe this deserves further research and correlation. After all, we are in the metaphysical sciences to utilize whatever works best under the circumstances. I'm glad we have Karen among our ranks and am thankful she has brought numerology forward into the 21st century arm in arm with astrology.

—EILEEN NAUMAN
Medical astrologer and
women's-fiction author

Introduction

Everyone wants to know more about themselves than they already seem to. Aren't you also just a touch more than curious about your future, love life, your dreams of success and fulfilling them? If so, then welcome to the wonderful world of Numerology, the Study of Numbers and their meanings. Just by knowing what a number represents and applying that information to your birth certificate name and birthdate, you can have the answers to those questions and curiosities. How to use this science of interpretation will be covered more specifically in Chapter 1.

For now, hello! I mean that sincerely to all of you number 8 people who have purchased this book. Why? Because the number 8 relates to business and career and that relates to money. Did I hit home? I also say hello to all of you number 5 individuals who may have purchased this book out of curiosity or suspicion and the hope of using this book for a "gambling" tool! As for you number 1 people; welcome to your new adventure and this field of research . . . you'll love it. I only hope you can stick with it long enough to get to the last chapter! Don't delegate this book to someone else to read and then have them fill you in on the details. To my number 3 and 6 friends: enjoy this book for the sake of your spouses, lovers, and friends. Help them begin helping themselves to a better future. If you want some detailed information to absorb, collect, and memorize, then I'm glad, number 2, you chose this book to flip through. Oh, and number 4 friends, don't get excited—this system is practical and not abstract. You can quit hesitating—go ahead and read the book. My intuitive number 7 and 9 friends want precision, intellect, and expanded awareness, and that is what you'll get.

I've described a tiny bit of each of the 9 prime digits of mathematics. In numerology, these prime digits become symbols that characterize your nature, actual patterns of human existence that allow you to be aware of events in your life.

You might already be asking, "What number am I?" I'll go into that very shortly, but first I'd like to say that with patience and practice on your part, this system will begin to clarify some questions you may have had about yourself and where you're headed.

Numerology, the modern-day term for the science of numbers, has been associated with the philosopher and mathematician, Pythagoras. However, many cultures throughout time have used both the practical and mystical understanding of numbers and their influences. Many references can be found, for example, from the Chaldeans, Egypt, Greece, Hebrews and others. References also occur in the Bible. In fact, it's fascinating that almost every sacred book since the dawn of time has made mention of the use of names, name changes, and understanding of the hidden meanings of numbers.

Believe me, knowing how to use and interpret the study of numbers is surprisingly accurate. Having your date of birth and full name allows you to pick up your own hammer and nails and build a life of security, happiness, and solutions.

To clarify what the numbers symbolize, let me tell you a little story:

In the beginning, there was the number 1. This number stands for man, the initiator, the leader, the independent individual. But man did not desire to remain on his own forever. Along came the number 2.

This number represents woman, the feminine receptor, number 1's helpmate, diplomat, and sensitive peacemaker. Both number 1 and number 2 decided it was time to marry and create a family. A child was born as an expression of the union of their love. Enter number 3. This number stands for the creative child, the mentally active and energetically imaginative expressor of goodwill and joy.

Now that the family was complete, all three numbers looked at each other and said, "We must build a house in which to live." Digging the earth for the foundation began. Voilà, number 4 was created, standing for discipline and the building of the foundation of things.

After the framework had been completed (number 4 requires step-by-step discipline and hard work), the family decided it was time to relax and recuperate from a job well done by taking vacation. They wanted to free themselves from the confines of limitation. Enter the number 5, which symbolizes freedom and the five senses. It communicates its desire and ideas through experiencing. Off the family went on a mini-vacation.

Back from their holiday, the family looked at the house they had just built. It was time to move in and make their house a home. That brought them to the number 6. This number represents domestic responsibilities, love, and harmony. It requires adjustment (of course, family arguments have to be resolved!) and community service. By expressing the number 6, the family realized they also had pets, neighbors, and community activities surrounding them. The family was pleased, happy for what they had accomplished and what they had to give and receive.

Yet the family realized there must be something more, and so there was. In walks number 7, which stands for analysis, wisdom, mental perfection, and faith. The family studied and wanted to learn more about themselves, the "whys" of their existence and their beliefs. They searched within themselves for the answers.

The family was again delighted after the lesson was complete, but in their reality, the facts came to the foreground. In order to live on this earth and survive, we must make a living, which requires choosing what is valued most, making decisions about the roles to play, and going out to establish a career to make the money desired. This leads to the number 8, which represents a blending together of spiritual and material beliefs and having ethics behind the decisions and careers chosen. It represents material aspects and value choices. It gives you what you deserve.

Going out into the world and accomplishing their goals of financial security as well as experiencing the joy of a task well done, the family recognized and was fascinated by the broad outlook they were beginning to manifest. Not only did they have a neighborhood to live in, but they were able to travel to different parts of the land, finding people like themselves with similar goals, desires, and experiences.

Recognizing this, the number 9 makes itself known. This number symbolizes a broad outlook. It is far reaching and can embrace people and places in all walks of life. It is the symbol of impersonal love and unity on a wide scale.

The family had come a long way. The road was challenging but well worth the effort, and the final destination had been reached. What was it they were learning to experience? LIFE ITSELF.

That's the end of the story of the nine prime digits of math. Let's go on to the first chapter and begin to see where you might go in the "wheel" of the universe.

I'VE GOT
YOUR NUMBER

1

Who Are You Anyway?

What number are you? I know this question has been on your mind since you decided to finish reading the introduction. So without further delay, I'll explain how to find the number that tells about you. This particular number is called the BIRTHPATH number. What is the Birthpath number? I'm glad you asked.

The Birthpath number symbolizes those inner traits and talents you're learning to develop. Like a diamond in the rough, the qualities that this number represents will be polished, defined, and accented by life's experiences. It's found by adding the month, day, and year you were born. In some cases you may hear it referred to as the Life Lesson number, School of Life number, or Birth Force number, but don't let that confuse you. Those names all describe the same thing—the *total of the birthdate*—and mean the same thing: quite simply, your *inner nature and your purpose in life*.

Let's take a look at the late, well-known composer, musician, and leader in the field of music, John Winston Lennon. This man was responsible for changing the history and style of music in the 1960s–70s. His birth date was October 9, 1940. To determine his Birthpath number, add the year of birth, the month of birth, and the day of birth vertically. This will give you the full value of the birthdate. Now reduce that number to a final digit. For example: October 9, 1940. October is the tenth month of the calendar year, so:

$$
\begin{array}{rl}
1940 & \text{year} \\
10 & \text{month} \\
\underline{9} & \text{day} \\
1959 & / 1 + 9 + 5 + 9 = 24 / 2 + 4 = 6 \text{ Birthpath}
\end{array}
$$

By the way, the year that you arrive at by adding up your birthdate is, was or will be a very important year for you. Check it out. For example, in 1959 John Lennon played in a group called Johnny and the Moondogs (along with Paul McCartney and George Harrison). Later that group's name was changed to The Silver Beatles and eventually The Beatles came into being. The rest is history. Now, what was important for you concerning the year you arrived at, or what might it be if it concerns the future? Think about it.

Remember, however, what we are concerned with at this point is the final digit. Always reduce compounds to a single digit, with the exception of the three compound numbers, 11, 22, and 33. These are called Master Numbers and have the potential of being twice as intense as their prime digit counterparts (2, 4, and 6). These particular compounds represent everything that the prime digit stands for with double the pressure and potential.

There is another way to add up the birth date, and that is to add the prime digits themselves. Let's take another example—July 4, 1948, the birthdate of a client and friend of mine.

$$
\begin{array}{l}
7/4/1948 \\
7 + 4 + 1 + 9 + 4 + 8 = 33 \\
3 + 3 = 6 \text{ Birthpath}
\end{array}
$$

These two ways, either the first method, which also tells you about one of your very important years, or the method shown above are the most accurate. Any other way, in this author's professional opinion, would only rationalize the truth to suit the needs of the moment.

In addition to the numbers 1–9, Pythagoras (the father of mathematics) considered the compound number 10, in and of itself, to be extremely important.

The number 10 relates to the higher vibration of the number 1 and indicates a beginning again, an emotional rebirth. It is the pioneer of new efforts on a higher level. It's like elevating the consciousness one octave. Although it is not generally considered a Master Number, you should still keep in mind what this compound represents as you reduce it to its prime digit.

Go ahead and add up your own birth date or the birth date of the person you'd like to know more about. Below is a description of the general type of each Birthpath number. In each explanation there are both positive and negative characteristics. Here, numbers are applied to human psychological conditions and traits, so people themselves can make things happen. The duality, therefore, will help you to see both sides of the picture more clearly.

Number One Birthpath

The number 1 represents natural leadership. Get out the raccoon hat, the sheepskin jacket, the rifle, and the backpack. Why? Because you're bound to blaze a trail into the unknown. There's a fire in your eyes for adventure when the mood strikes and when the wind is at your back. Generally, you're not the type to shrink from responsibility or the unknown. You have your own set of convictions, ideals, and morals.

These ideologies may not be considered the "norm," but nevertheless, they are your law. Furthermore, all those whom you consider friends and associates had better abide by those rules. You have excellent judgment and a desire to push ahead in life. You don't follow; you're meant to lead. Although you appear easy-going and open-minded, once a person gets to know you, they recognize the initiative in your nature, that part of you that needs to forge ahead.

This sense of enterprise may have lain dormant during the earlier years. During those times, it may have seemed very natural for you to want a family and homelife complete with picket fence and rosebushes. However, try to be careful not to rush into marriage. Very often during the middle twenties to early thirties, those needs change. This transition of ideas, especially if you're a 1 woman who happens to be married prior to that time, may cause some problems in a marriage that happens too soon in life. It's not uncommon for you to change paddles quickly while going upstream.

I say this because you are quite impulsive on occasion. You may act first and think later. A 1 man or woman might end up going through the "school of hard knocks" when it really isn't necessary because he or she jumps the gun. Yes, you are impatient and would like to take action instantly, but allowing a little more time to think things through will help you climb to the top of the mountain that much more easily.

Challenge and the accomplishment of your goals can be as natural to you as water is to the flower. You may reassure the less aggressive and less independent types or become irritated by their indecisiveness. When you do decide to strive to the top of the ladder, it may just be to see if you can do it.

You forge ahead. What's interesting is that once success has been achieved, you may drop your claim, walking away and putting stakes down somewhere else. Just when that ball of success was rolling nicely along, you may feel the need to toss it to another court and begin again.

But for every positive, there is a negative as well. When feeling less than confident, you may not want to take up any challenge at all! There may be a million and one excuses for why you shouldn't take action or proceed with a new venture, but it's not easy to fool yourself. Your intuition operates within you like a steering wheel trying to turn you in the right direction.

Whether you like it or not, you won't be allowed to lag behind. You're here to stand up and be counted. If you won't choose it of your own free will, life itself and its experiences will force you to take the lead in some way at a point during your life. Think you are not ready? Smile—you really are. Just give yourself half a chance to prove it.

You have a natural exuberance and do not like being stuck in a rut. That makes you pace like a restless wildcat and could also cause your temper to flare up. Yes, I did mention a temper. When really stirred up, cherry-bomb explosions seem mild next to your display of emotion. Thank goodness it usually doesn't last long, nor do you always recall what caused the outburst in the first place.

This sense of independence rules the roost for you as well. You secretly want to be the king or queen of your own castle. However, when family discussions do arise, you won't thump your rod of power blatantly. You will try to see all sides of the issue before passing judgment. Your spouse or lover should try to show you the necessary affection and devotion coupled with an admiring loyalty. Do remember that when the shoe's on the other foot, those feelings extended to you should be reciprocated. You should never be too busy for that.

When proper balance of thought and action are established, gratification, recognition, and true independence and leadership become rewards for the effort you have exerted. If you learn to recognize those negative traps of bossiness, arrogance, or narrow-mindedness and not to fall into their net, you will be on your way. The world and all that's in it can be yours.

Number Two Birthpath

Have you ever seen a human file drawer of knowledge full of information regarding the "little things"? Well, look in the mirror; it's you. You are a collector and gatherer of information useful to any endeavor you wish to undertake. You're the type who can gather all those little details that others may have missed, absorbing like a sponge what's going on around you.

It's not the grandiose that can be so important or means that much to you, either. It's the small things that matter most. Others grow to realize that even the smallest sign of gratitude cast in your direction or the simplest gesture of thanks given to you in appreciation can mean the world to you.

Being sensitive and striving toward objectivity will help you to employ your power of mediation. You are diplomatic, carrying with you a spark of charm, wit, and subtle cleverness. When getting ahead in life, you can succeed in your goals without stepping on someone else's toes to do it. There is a strong innate desire to please, to bring everything and everybody together in harmony. This blessing you possess can also be a burden in disguise. Trying to make everyone happy, without recognizing your own needs or sacrificing your desires and opinions just to keep peace, can lead to vacillation, uncertainty, or lack of self-confidence. Then the "Henry Kissinger" in you becomes the "Humpty-Dumpty," and you will sit on a fence unable to make up your mind.

When employing your art of persuasion, you won't always come directly to the point, but you won't lie either. This is especially true if someone asks your opinion about something that you know might hurt their feelings. You may diplomatically beat around the bush, softening the blow here and there, cushioning what you need to say. In the end, you get your point across.

The number 2 in this position indicates that yours is a delicate inner nature that is coupled with flashes of intuition. Like antennae cast out to probe the perimeter, you easily pick up the vibrations of others. You may have a tendency to wear your heart on your sleeve more than you would like to admit. The less attuned can easily bruise you through harsh words or coarse gestures. It is at those times, when buried hurt or frustration have not been released, that you can be subject to mood swings. These emotional fluctuations can make you feel as if you are riding on a seesaw of highs and lows. Emotional balance, the even flow of feeling, is one of the things you are here to master and control. Don't hold back, but do balance the bridle.

Since your desire for peace and harmony is strong, you will be the first to give in when an argument starts. It is clear to you that fighting solves nothing and no real winner emerges from discord. The irony is that you want peace at all costs, even if it takes war to attain it.

The charm and poise you possess may bring the opposite sex around you, desiring your soft attentions. In love and marriage, you're extremely attentive, affectionate, and loyal. You are the woman behind the man or the man behind the woman. You will be there to give the necessary advice, confidence, and support to the ones you love. And all the while, you are making the home a haven of relaxation and comfort, painting pictures of the soft breeze of serenity and contented companionship.

It's best for you to be involved with people who share the ideals you possess. At times, your road of life is crossed with situations that deal with women, partnerships, and working in groups, all of which require the tools of arbitration, emotional balance, and objectivity. These traits are natural to you and should be developed to the fullest. Finally, share with those friends and acquaintances you meet the knowledge, charm, and inner calm you possess. You'll be rewarded twofold.

Number Three Birthpath

You have an inner childlike innocence and curiosity that just may keep you forever young. What you appreciate most in others is a sense of humor and an optimistic outlook. On this path, the need to recognize that "in every gray cloud there is a silver lining" is most important.

Naturally, keeping your "sunnier side up" at times may not be easy. Your normally easy smile can, on occasion, turn into one big frown. When this happens, your optimism may turn into worry instead. Did I say worry? This is a word you usually try to avoid in your vocabulary. You may constantly remind your friends and acquaintances that there's nothing to worry about because life's too short. Anxiety in your book doesn't solve anything. Oh, yes, you're a wonderful preacher about worry and its pitfalls. Too bad you don't always practice what you preach. You will very rarely show it, but you may fret more than anyone would guess.

When you keep your positive outlook shining strongly, you can be a walking reflection of imagination and vision. You color most of what you do with a flair for the dramatic. When you send out the rays of hope and that sunny smile, people gravitate to you like bees to honey.

I'll bet you never realized that when others come to you and pour out their troubles, they walk away feeling better. Most of it has to do with the way you handle these situations. No, you may not have expelled great words of wisdom or even gotten to the "root" of the problem, although you are quite capable of doing both. Your gift of gab, your sense of humor, and your ability to see the foibles of a bad situation are what lift and encourage others. Somehow when people seek out your solace, they feel that no matter how bad the situation, you show them a ray of sunshine.

You do have a gift for words. In fact, anything that

allows for creative expression, whether it be a hobby or career, should be pursued. You can paint flowery pictures with either your words or your actions. With this gift, you can coddle, cuddle, and bloom the buds of success for yourself and others. You can make a fine writer or lecturer, for example, if these qualities are developed.

Wait a minute. I can hear it already. You might be thinking or saying out loud, "I'm not that talented. I can't even draw a straight line or write a letter without changing it at least once. How can I be that creative?" You're just letting your inner lack of self-worth pop out again. This is truly an unfounded fear. What you think you are capable of doing and what you actually are able to produce may not be one and the same.

Deep within your nature is the desire for center stage and the limelight. Among loved ones and friends and in the comforts of your social circle, the "ham" in you emerges. You'd like to entertain and amuse and receive the applause of recognition and appreciation when you've done a good job.

This same sense of appreciation extends to those you love. You usually enjoy being pampered, hugged, and told how much you're cared for. When it comes to receiving presents from friends and family, you're like a little child. You are bubbly and exuberant as you enjoy the pleasures of gift giving and receiving; there is a special place in your heart for Christmas, birthdays, and all special occasions.

There are a few things to keep in mind as you travel along the road of life. Once you start a project or endeavor, make sure you complete it. You can be notorious for scattering your energies and talents if you don't keep on top of things. Try to avoid the pitfalls of selfishness and temper eruptions. Yes, when you're angry you can exhibit childish temper tantrums and may not hesitate to throw things in reaction to your frustration. This could lead to the "give me" syndrome, wanting everything done your way and only for yourself. A 3's sense of self-esteem when out of control can be likened to riding a horse without a bridle. The only way to end, in that case, would be on the ground and not in the saddle of balance. Always strive to express what you are and what you feel with continued vision, a sense of humor, and an optimistic outlook.

The number 3 represents fertility, children, and expansion. You may enjoy children immensely. You can communicate with the young in a very special manner and are able to reach them in a way that others may not. Generally speaking, you can swing up to intellectual heights or down to simple and childlike satisfactions, knowing how to understand and appreciate both extremes.

Finally, there is a latent potential in your nature to quite naturally develop your clairvoyant ability. This talent may lead to curiosity involving the metaphysical world. Keep in tune with the positive and trust your intuitive hunches. Use your gift for the betterment of all concerned and you could be of great service.

Number Four Birthpath

Perfecting the practical and courting common sense are two of the natural traits you possess and ones you will be developing to the fullest. When was the last time you weren't practical or wished to be more logical? Not only do you have a natural talent for discipline, you have the ability to produce long-lasting results for your efforts. Slow and sure, steady and secure, is how you like the rudder of your ship guided. Secretly, you would rather do things yourself, thus being assured that the job gets done. I've seen more than just a few 4s get upset if a task, errand, or project wasn't completed in the exact fashion it was explained.

At times you may have to enter the classroom of hard knocks in order to learn when and when not to let go. You may be tenacious with possessions and with people, clinging to the very roots that may have outgrown the soil in which they were placed. Tried and true is fine, but latching onto security purely for security's sake alone is another matter. Life's experiences will show you the difference between stick-to-itiveness and being stuck in a rut.

In relationships, you're dependable and wholesome and as loyal as the day is long. In the beginning, it may take some time before you decide to call someone else your confidant, friend, and/or mate. You're usually cautious in your attitude and prefer to take things one step at a time to develop your allegiances.

The family is important to you; however relatives and in-laws can be the pain instead of the pleasure in your haven of security if they begin butting in rather than helping out. Woe to the kin who crosses that line of distinction. Overall, you do want to see your loved ones happy and most of all secure.

Caring for those you love may mean making sure they eat right, get enough rest, and keep bundled up nice and warm in cold weather. You express your devotion in logical and practical ways, providing common-sense security and courtesy to those you love.

The only drawbacks to your gestures of tenderness might be that you restrict the emotional side too much and may even hide it altogether. You don't lay flowery metaphors at someone's feet. You provide stability instead. Do try to keep in mind, though, that in close emotional relationships, both words and actions are required. Don't be stingy in the verbal expression of your affections.

Holding in your feelings and waiting too long to release frustrations and tension or even overexuberant joy can cause all sorts of problems. Anxiety may mount until you worry about everything. Tension could become trapped within the physical body causing such things as muscle aches and pains, and possibly back or stomach problems. As you can see, holding back emotions might not be such a healthy idea.

Abrupt words, pushy people, or hasty actions just

make you even more stubborn. Taken to extremes, the fixedness you possess can turn into narrow-mindedness. The more someone else tries to "con" you into making decisions or doing deeds before you see fit to do so, the more you'll resist and shut the big oak door of inflexibility behind you.

Finally, the simple pleasures mean the most. You're basically the "au naturel" type. For example, a home-cooked meal prepared with love but not extravagance is really appreciated. Gourmet dinners with impressive French names are fine, but if you don't like the way it looks, you won't eat it. You like the outdoors and being close to nature in all its splendor and majesty. Hiking, bike riding, canoeing, etc., can be a part of your need to get back to the basics. Overall, you are of the earth and belong to the rich soil of durability, patience, and perseverance.

Number Five Birthpath

I haven't met a 5 yet who didn't like to travel, even if it's only to take occasional short-distance trips. Staying put for too long a time is not your idea of fun. Freedom, in almost every sense, is what this number is all about. Communication and progress are attributes that are a part of your natural makeup.

You can be a trendsetter, an innovative individual who likes to talk, satisfy your curiosities, and produce results of which you can be proud. When you've done a good job, like a proud peacock you'll spread the feathers of your own special flash and style in satisfaction. There is a bit of a flaw in this area of accomplishment. During the climb to freedom and success, you can become extremely sensitive to criticism in conversation. One would never know it, because your quick responses and confident actions make others believe you can take it. Surprise! Underneath that mentally active and pliable facade lies an easily offended nature.

Your natural zest for life and living will be contagious to others you meet. They can feel that energetic aura all around you, no matter how subtly it permeates the air or how dynamically it comes across. This attitude also helps you to remain lighthearted and easily adaptable. You are subject to mood shifts, but they very rarely last long. And if an argument should occur, you can forget about it as quickly as it came about. Normally, you won't hold grudges.

Keeping physically fit is also important. When you've noticed the scales tipping a bit to the opposite direction, you're not the type to just talk about taking the pounds off, you'll actually begin doing something about it—right then. Activities like jogging, dance classes, horseback riding, etc., are some of the things you may engage in to keep you in shape.

The 5 is another of those numbers that doesn't want to wait until tomorrow for what it can do today. If restricted, you could develop a biting sarcasm and lose your sparkle. If you had your way, the words *hemmed in* would never be practiced, let alone defined and described in *Webster's Dictionary*. Naturally, you recognize that having your roots is quite necessary, and establishing a foundation and secure base gives you the stability you seek. Even the birds up in the sky come home to roost. Being tied down or trapped in a consistent maze of routine in your professional and personal life will upset your emotional and mental state of wellbeing. But even that wouldn't last too long anyway. In the end, you usually figure out a way to slip out from under the noose.

The opposite sex is generally attracted to the 5 quite easily. This magnetism, in part, stems from an inner charisma and a quick-draw type of wit. When it's time for permanency, you should choose your spouse carefully. Your present or potential partner should understand that you are not really the nine to five type of person who enjoys regular routines, like having dinner every day promptly at six thirty P.M. Your mate should also be a friend and lover with an accent on the word *friend*!

Others learn to expect the unexpected in you. They look in one place for you and find you somewhere else instead. You're not the type to carry on lengthy conversations regarding just one topic, either. No, you can cover a variety of subjects in just a short time. It's also difficult for others to match wits with you and keep up. Listen, once your resources are tapped, you can sell an igloo to an Eskimo if you put your mind to it. One of the best defenses you may have is the words you speak. If slighted, your silver-coated tongue turns into a blade of steel in disguise, which you won't think twice about using if you feel you are being intentionally put down.

When burning the candle at both ends, so to speak, or not handling your personal freedom properly, you can seem to develop a "drifter" type of syndrome. You may roll with the tide and throw the dice of life. When lacking roots, you may become extremely impulsive, self-centered, and rather jealous of another's successes.

You have the talent of winning over others to your side without having to boast or boost your own ego to do it. This success hinges on how much you have perfected your charm, good manners, and mental agility. It also depends on how well you've molded your inner magnetism. Most of your knowledge is gained through experience rather than from books, and life is your teacher. If you haven't opened the classroom door, now is the time to do it!

Number Six Birthpath

You've got a talent for making someone else feel right at home. In fact, your home is where your heart lies even if away from it for a period of time. Whether it's entertaining a large gathering or having a conversation over a cup of coffee with a friend, there is a warm and caring interest that you extend.

One of the smaller yet very necessary ways to show

your concern is through the meals you serve. You could be the type to place food out on the table when friends stop over or neighbors pay a visit. Speaking of sustenance, you could win the Betty Crocker Bake-Off or be given the compliment of Master Chef on more than one occasion. A 6 usually has that knack for preparing scrumptious delights. When you've got the time, you'll use that talent and create meals that are not only lovely to look at, but delicious too.

You are considered the humanitarian, lending that helping hand to those in need. You'll stick with the underdog long after everyone else seems to have given up, even if you need to sacrifice yourself to do it. This is a very commendable quality, but one that also deserves a word of caution. In your patronage and cloak of caring, you need to discern when to give, how much, and to whom. If you don't remain objective, those you take under your wing with zealous inspiration and a concerned attitude will turn into associations of burden and much frustration.

Part of this potential problem stems from putting people on pedestals on which they don't belong. You give much and expect much, if not more, in return. So you may guide, motivate, and try to inspire those into the image you know they can portray. The difficulty is, they may not want to be what you expect them to be. The key words for your path are service with a smile, learning to adjust your affairs to suit the needs of others, and acceptance. Give of your wise advice only when asked. It's at those times you'll know that what you say will be appreciated and really heard, and the expenditure of energy it may take will be worth the effort.

I haven't met a 6 yet who isn't somewhat "parental" with people and pets. You can pick up small stray animals and take care of them. You might visit the zoo in the springtime, for example, to see all the new little baby creatures being born. The "little ones," both animal and human, have a special place in your heart.

Your own children will be cherished greatly. Prior

to the time they begin grappling with, challenging, and living life on their own, you will try to do everything possible to prepare them. When the inevitable does arrive and your young have to spread their wings to fly, it may be a little harder for you than most to let go without feeling a little saddened. If the parental instinct goes beyond what it should, you can become possessive with those you love.

As a lover or mate, you're loyal to house and spouse. You seek to find a partner who is stable, humorous, and polished. In marriage, you want to know that you will be financially secure enough to enjoy a few comforts along the way. You seem to feel more complete if you have someone with whom to share your life. Yet, here is the irony: the standards you set may be so high when in search of the ideal mate that you may have problems establishing the type of permanent relationship you desire. Even though the number 6 represents marriage and the home and hearth, you could remain single. Again, it goes back to pedestals of perfection as opposed to the reality of acceptance.

Others shouldn't be fooled by your seemingly patient, calm, and refined charm. Underneath lurks an emotional time bomb! When happy and content, you can purr like a kitten. When feeling frustrated, unappreciated, or loaded down with too much responsibility with no end in sight, those around you should beware. On some occasions it would be better if they headed for the hills. Hiding behind a rock could be a much safer place than facing the emotional display you can deliver. Not to worry, you'll calm down again. Generally, it's not your style to let crude or uncontrolled behavior totally overcome your nature.

You can be appreciative of the classical and creative arts. At some point in your life, you will be involved in a field of service where you can employ your ideals, express your appreciations, and make the world a better place in which to live.

Number Seven Birthpath

Knowledge is truth, and probing to find it uncovers solutions. You're the one who asks the questions; however, you may not like questions asked of you, especially if they are considered your own personal and private business. Generally, you're not satisfied merely to know *what* is going on, you want to know *why*. This searching for information makes you excellent at investigation and specialization along unusual and nontraditional lines of endeavor. In fact, some of your successes might depend on an effort that is out of the ordinary.

Although you may be considered a lone wolf, relying upon yourself for your entertainment and activities, you may still depend on others more than you might like to admit. You will tell others how you can get along very nicely alone, when secretly, you could fear being lonely.

Mental camaraderie is important when you select your friends and loved ones. You try to choose allies with whom you share the same level of thinking. Unlike the 6 who expects emotional perfection, you seek to find the perfect intellectual companion.

Deep down you are extremely sensitive, but you lock that well of emotion behind the doors of reason and analytical rationalization. You may feel that when emotions get in the way, your thinking capacity and rationality go right down the drain, washed away by your watery feelings. Your best tactic of defense is silence before expressing your feelings, so that you have the time to go within and control the emotional turmoil you might be feeling.

There is an inner need here for solitude, getting away from the maddening crowd and the hustle and bustle. You really dislike noise and confusion, particularly in the home. Music that is too loud, the television blasting, and the phone ringing, all at the same time, can disrupt your thoughts and make you quite nervous; therefore, you enjoy the peacefulness that nature provides. Living outside a busy metropolis is recommended. If you can't do that, get out to the country more often and take walks near the seashore or give your home decor a sense of the peaceful outdoors. These calming settings will give you an instant boost and bring your inner rudder back to balance.

Time itself is important to you. You don't like wasting it on frivolity. This isn't to imply, however, that you don't like to entertain or be entertained, because you do. In fact, you may have been known to paint the town red on occasion. The difference is that you're selective as to where and when.

You like to be complimented (don't we all?!), but you could find yourself falling for false flattery or praise that might lead you into encounters that are not sincere. At times you may not recognize a bad situation until you're in it. Although you are extremely intuitive, you could rationalize your way out of listening to that intuition. Then, before you know it, a wrong turn has been taken. The more you experience life and grow to rely on that still, small voice, the less likely you are to fall prey to illusionary circumstance.

Others may see you as aloof and just a touch mysterious. That makes you even more intriguing, especially to the opposite sex. The outward chivalrous grace you possess can charm someone right around your little finger. Ah, you are a master at disguise! Why? Because underneath the veiled enchantment lies a pool of picky perfection.

Once you are hooked, flirting outside the relationship rarely occurs unless you have the notion that the grass is greener on the other side of the fence. Yes, it always *seems* greener in the other meadow, but look again and be very certain. Overall, you are very loyal to the ones you love, not wanting to tempt fate and potentially lose the good things you've found.

Intuition does guide the number 7 like a gyroscope.

There is another side to your analytical nature that deals with inner wisdom and cosmic law. On the everyday level, you may have a hand in politics, technical research of some sort, or the law. On the other side, you may seek information regarding religions, philosophies, creative specialties or the principles of cosmology. You have a deep awareness of spirit, sometimes more than even your own cool analytical mind will realize.

Number Eight Birthpath

You are energized, dynamic, and carry with you a natural executive authority. Yours is the ability to command and control and to influence others with what you say and do. Hello to you, Mr. or Ms. "Dynamo."

Naturally, you're not that obvious with the power you possess, but it can be felt nonetheless. Unlike the number 1 who aggressively strives to the top for the sake of the challenge, you can soar to heights for the value of the return on your time and investment. Once you get there, you will very rarely hop onto a new bandwagon. You'll extend and expand what you already have.

If you desire to take the steps necessary to succeed in a career endeavor, donning a confident and successful image is important to you. People who have gained symbols of success such as a fine home, new car, diplomas, and degrees will impress you because those things stand for accomplishment.

Now, I realize that you are not one of the most patient individuals, but when it's time to dig in your heels, you will. You may not be that patient, but you are enduring.

To get where you want to go may take time and some repeated effort. With this number, you get exactly what you deserve. Sometimes you'd rather delegate than do yourself what is necessary. You can handle the extra pressure it takes to build your empire, whatever that might mean to you. The rewards you receive will be in direct proportion to the effort extended.

Another thing that will allow you to survive some of those vital repeated attempts is that competitive spirit you have. Whether blatantly obvious or not, you don't like to lose or be delayed. Games, sports, hobby, or career—once you're involved, it's all the way and then some.

In the home, you may be the delegator of the family and be quite organized in doing so. A woman who is an 8, for example, may claim she has a "system"; so don't ruin it. Also, she's the type who really appreciates being married to a mate who can do the cooking—maybe even a little more often than she does.

Love plays an important part in your life, and you have a way of sizing up personal relationships quite quickly. It's either playing the field (until you find what you like) or a relationship with one person that could last a lifetime.

Because you prefer to hold the passion of love behind closed doors and want to keep your personal business to yourself, you're not openly affectionate in public. You don't always say what you really feel about the one you love, but it can be seen anyway. All your mate has to do is glance into your eyes. There's a sparkle and a penetrating look so loving and passionate, words need not be expressed. An 8 can pierce or praise with just a gaze.

Did you know you talk in tangents on occasion? You don't think so? Ask the one who listens to you regularly. Your thoughts may not always complete themselves as you speak. Or while you're discussing one subject, you start thinking about another one and voice it at the same time. And there stands whoever is listening, confused and having to ask you to repeat yourself or start from the beginning. Don't worry though; it's just a sign that you're always thinking.

The less than ideal side of you will be concerned with making a quick buck, selfish schemes, and shrewd methods of acquiring power. By the way, that word *power* can excite you into attaining it or make you shy away. Also, when overly concerned with and pushing to gain, you may place a dollar amount on every single thing you do, putting more emphasis on the money than on the accomplishment and recognition that can be gained. These negative traps should be avoided and sidestepped as quickly as possible. Even though the right way may be the longer way, the reward you receive when you get there will be unmatched.

You are here to develop and perfect your sense of faith and ethics behind all your business dealings and personal relationships. That means keeping one foot in the spiritual realm and one foot in the material realm, blending the two together in perfect harmony. Consequently, at some point in your life, regardless of what else you might be doing, you'll search for an even better understanding of the cosmos and higher law. You may become interested in the occult, different philosophies or religions, the meaning of life and death, and the evolutionary cycle of things. Through the experiences of both the material and the spiritual, you begin to see the value of doing what's best not only for yourself, but for all concerned.

An 8 who has worked to reach the top of the ladder is really a sight to see. You will then deserve the proper power, financial security, authority, and successful image that was promised.

Number Nine Birthpath

You are generous, impressionable, and at times, a dreamer of the impossible dream. You see the world as it ought to be, not as it really is. This number stands for a broadened outlook and is generally considered the number of completion and universality. It is not unusual to note that a 9 may seem to possess a touch of every other number's qualities in it.

My, my, aren't you complex?! Not really; just misunderstood on occasion, because others may try to pigeonhole the qualities you possess. The truth is you can play any role you want with those you love and with whom you associate. You color yourself and your attitudes like a chameleon to suit the situation or the person, and blend in comfortably. You do this in order to harmonize, help, and guide those around you. Is that sneaky? No, just well-rounded and attuned to the sensitivities of others. You do this not to camouflage or offend, but to enhance the circumstances. You can adopt the opinions, attitudes, and even life-styles of those around you.

You are here to expand your knowledge, broaden your horizons, and see the value in all walks of life. You have not been put here to limit your experiences. Life itself will see to that.

Some, for example, may see you as the one who puts on rose-colored glasses, viewing situations and people from too idealistic a state. This can be true. When the need arises either for you to "get away" from harshness, or when it's necessary to prove a point in regard to the limits people put on themselves, you'll don your "shades." You hide then, incognito, behind philosophies of what you know should be but, in fact, are not. Others may see you as the person who dreams of fairy-tale princes, princesses, kings, and queens. To those, you seem nebulous, and they can't quite hold on to or grasp the essence of you very easily.

To them it's like trying to hold water in the palm of the hand; it runs right through their fingers. Well, that's what they get for trying to possess you, mold you into their own special perceptions, or for not wanting to reach upward to your level of thinking. These people will attempt to hang on but can't. I can't blame them much for trying. When using your abilities to the fullest and to the best, you are quite a catch.

There are still others who see you as a fighter for a cause or a traveler who wants to visit faraway places, either through vacation or career. They see you as a person involved with the public, whether it be teaching, creating, working in a service business, or just simply being acquainted with a variety of different people you've met along the way. This is true also. What's the reality then? All of the above.

Through your experiences and gained knowledge you will be called to serve the public at one time or the other. When acting positively, you're not hung up on claiming a special identity, although that often happens without your even trying, because of what you may do. Nor will you exhibit the personal and selfish side; you're simply impersonal and objective, reaching out beyond the boundaries and acting accordingly for those in need.

Yes, I know learning the lesson of impersonal love and broad perspective may not be easy at first. During the earlier years, you may have already learned the hard way what those qualities mean and how to apply them. This could have included separations of sorts, setbacks or delays, all of which affected your emotions greatly and taught you that clinging too close will limit your growth. For example, if you think possessing lots of money is equal to security, chances are you won't have very much. Why? Because you have concentrated solely on one idea and cannot see beyond the material realm. You should leave the monetary concerns up to the 8s (barring the reality of knowing you have to pay bills, take care of your own, etc.) and concentrate more on people. Through serving the people in some way, you will help to create the prosperity you desire.

Yes, you are a humanitarian, but you are one with reservations. Unlike a 6 who will give possibly to its detriment, you will lend your helping hand and advice as long as you know others will then begin to help themselves. If not, you won't stay around for too long, allowing them to use you as a leaning post in an attempt to make changes.

The negative side of your nature may include fickleness, moodiness, greed, and/or an explosive temper that harbors a rebellious and pessimistic attitude about life. These traits will occur when you worry too much about your image, a love gone sour or how to get along in the material world. When you lack direction, you may tend to know a little about everything and a whole lot about nothing.

The 9 is the number of worldly experiences. Consequently during the early adult years, you might be a jack-of-all-trades until you find your niche, which usually occurs around middle to late twenties.

Number Eleven Birthpath

You can either whimsically wile away the hours in amusing chitchat or seriously guide, inspire, and motivate others to greater achievements.

You do learn quickly. In fact, some of you may have a touch of mental genius in some area or other. No one has to tell you more than once to do something, barring those few occasions when the message will need to be repeated. Your attention span can be long or short depending on your mood or interest in what others have to say. You, like the number 9, can appear to be listening to every word that is being said, when in reality you're a million miles away. You can swing 180 degrees to the left of the topic being discussed.

You are considered a little high-strung and appear to have quite a bit more nervous energy than your counterpart, number 2. It may be hard for you to sit still, for example, without changing positions at least once during a short span. But you'll swear that you're the calmest person around, moving at a snail's pace. The problem is, a snail's pace to you is really a road-runner's tempo to someone else!

You can sway from mood to mood. You are aware of it and don't really like it in yourself. The moodiness stems from your extremely sensitive and emotional nature. There are times when the slightest remark made (unintentional or otherwise) could start you crying buckets. Obviously this aspect pertains to women in general, but it is not uncommon for an 11 male to let his eyes well up with water when sadness or a stressful situation becomes apparent.

Yes, you are sensitive and a little more idealistic than you would like to admit, too. You may shed a tear (although you might try to hide it) when watching a romantic story on television, experiencing the loss or injury of a pet, or watching the bride walk down the aisle on the day of her wedding. The romantic within you rings strong and clear tones.

When love strikes the right chord, it's a sight to behold. You become excited, exuberant, and even a bit childlike over the jubilation of finding your match. The stars are in your eyes, and you can appear as if you are walking on air. Outwardly, you may try to maintain some semblance of composure to hide some of that exuberance, but deep down you know you can't contain it, and the bubbles of rapture pop out to show the world how you feel.

When attached, you are considered the inspiration behind your mate. You give courage, comfort, and emotional security to the family and strive to keep the peace. I've seen more than one number 11 put aside personal goals for the sake of the growth of the immediate family. This could be a dedicated quality or a deadly detriment. Like the numbers 6 and 9, you can be used as a doormat (either knowingly or unknowingly) by others if you wear your heart on your sleeve without the cloak of objectivity.

When negative in thoughts or action and feeling less than confident, you can be a procrastinator. You can hem and haw in giving an opinion or advice. When not sure of your goals, you can drain others of energy and time in a futile attempt to solve self-inflicted or imaginary problems.

When positive and moving upward, you have the ability to motivate and guide others to greater successes without receiving the same in return. On acting positively, you won't expect to be matched measure for measure in what you give and receive, but through your efforts others begin to recognize what you've done for them and for the most part, return the recognition and applause in your direction.

You can be a very spiritual individual, full of inspiration, vision, talent, and gifted ideas. You can be the achiever of fame if it is not sought from ulterior motives. You raise your torch and can bring light into darkness, brightening the path of others.

Number Twenty-Two Birthpath

The stoic and the tower of strength are attributes that describe your inner nature. You won't budge an inch on principle, refusing to be swayed in loyalty or from what you know is right. This is an admirable quality most of the time, but it can cause you problems.

Instead of bending like a willow, you prefer to stand like an oak. You appear to stand straight and tall, almost defiant against the possibility of becoming weather-beaten. When you turn around, you notice that some of your bark has been chipped away and you've been scarred because of your unwillingness to be more flexible. Basically, you are here to learn when to let go of what is no longer useful and has outgrown its purpose, and when to secure those things that are useful.

You are very selective in friendships. One shouldn't try to force an alliance with you. It may take weeks or even months, but you will be the one to decide who is a friend and who is not. Others will be able to feel your stable presence and your inner strength. They will either feel extremely comfortable around you or not at ease at all. They sense that around you they will have to know what it is they are talking about and do so in a logical fashion. Others will not be able to fluff their way through for long. It only takes once, sometimes twice, for you to see through the facade and make an immediate judgment. If you ever get the wrong impression of someone else, it's very difficult for you to change your mind.

You can be true-blue, even when it hurts. The only time you may have a love affair on the side is if you've entered into a relationship prematurely or for some reason because you've felt you had to seek temporary solace elsewhere. Even then, it's a rare occurrence.

Ending unhappy marriages or romantic affairs is never easy, but it is especially difficult for you. You can be the last of the true chivalrists who basically believe in tradition, ceremony, and the family unit staying intact. Once a commitment is made, you would like to think it will last a lifetime; therefore, you should be especially careful in whom you choose and what you want out of life. Once the foundation is set, the concrete may be hardened into permanency because of your feelings and beliefs.

You are considered the Master Builder on the material plane. Your scope can be far-reaching, if you want it to be, in whatever field of endeavor you choose. You need to be aware and yet cautious of your talent for soaring to the peak of the mountain. As quickly as you can fly to the top and secure your position, you can plummet back down again. Concerning yourself with too fixed an attitude or anything other than strong and reliable ethics could find you unleashing upon others a dominating and dictatorial rule. This behavior could give you the undesirable reputation as a master at underhanded schemes.

On the positive side, you have the most potential for the mastery of making your dreams come true. Your steps will be slow and sure when implementing those masterful plans and huge ideas. You calculate your every move by plotting plans A, B, and C. This way if one formula fails, you have alternatives to rely on. Couple this with your ability to think bigger than the norm and you can create a conglomerate of successes for the betterment of all. If you do it right, the foundation you've laid will bring you long-lasting success.

No cracks or crevices will be seen to shake the structure from its roots.

Number Thirty-Three Birthpath

You can make friends and acquaintances quite easily, and this includes the opposite sex as well. The attraction does not necessarily relate to sexual magnetism. It focuses on being the confidant and companion; others feel as if they can pour their heart out and you will listen.

The parental aspect is also strong. Your care and concern may not restrict itself just to your immediate surroundings. From relative to friend to mere acquaintance, your patronage extends outward. The whole world, in a sense, can be your child!

You may have a little trouble developing the kinds of personal relationships you really desire. For example, what would normally start off as a dating romance may end up as something a little different. If you will look back on past relationships, you will notice that more than one of your romantic encounters turned out to be one of deeply platonic ties, not sexual liaisons or romantic raptures. You may have ended up parenting or counseling, not playing the role of lover.

Highly charged and emotional, you are quick-witted, playful, and expressively talented. You may be involved in more than one community organization or associations of service, juggling your time and energy like a circus act to meet your commitments. The home means much to you as well, and although you will not spend all your hours in that domain (on occasion you may not be there at all), the security of your haven is important. Like the number 6, you feel others ought to do what you say because you know what is right and usually you are accurate. On occasion you'll need to temper your opinions by not pushing or meddling in the affairs of those closest to you.

In romantic involvements, you can be in love with

two totally different types of individuals at the same time—one from a distance and one nearby. Someone else may wonder if this is possible. Maybe not for the average person, but in the case of a 33 I'm not talking about the average, ordinary person.

Great game players on the dating scene, you are cardholders who know all the tricks to use so that you can add up the points, employ your ace in the hole, and end up the victor. Once you're caught, you can assume a much different role.

Although still active, humorous, and alert to outside commitments, you will seem to settle down a little more than your mate may have first anticipated while dating you. You'll put on the cap of responsibility and gladly accept your role as mate. In fact, you may even be more of the homebody than you want to appear to be, because underneath it all, a meaningful marriage is most important to you.

You can be moody, nervous, sarcastic, or cold when not in an optimistic frame of mind. This will manifest itself if you feel unloved or unappreciated. When confused, you are like a bee buzzing around trying to find honey in a dessert, frantically searching but bewildered as to which direction to go in.

If allowed to open up early in life and to experience various facets of knowledge and to move out of the emotional security of the family unit, you can be quite broad in your outlook on life later on. Elevating the consciousness, you can be considered the Master Teacher, guiding others by practicing what you preach and not merely talking about it.

2

What Are You Like on the Job?

In today's demanding world, no one can really afford to ignore the basic necessities of life. The vast majority of the population works for a living in order to reach the goals they have set for themselves.

Jobs, careers, and professions are an integral part of our existence. What will you be like as you work your way up? How will your boss get along with you? What kind of an employer would you be? Check your Birthpath number below to recognize your talents on the job.

Number One Employee

You're applauded for the ability to work alone. A 1 employee will make decisions or handle a problem without feeling that checking with the boss is always necessary. Many times, you'll handle a new job on your own without being shown the ropes or without being trained. You are an initiator. You make decisions and act on them quickly, very rarely looking back over your shoulder.

It's hard for you to tolerate being held back (unless you have a 4 or 6 totaling the birth name; see Chapter

4). You expect recognition when deserved and need to be able to express your opinions rather than just do what you are told. Your employer needs to encourage originality in thought and action, and offer the opportunity for advancement.

Number One Employer

You love the challenge of leadership. When working, you rule the roost, energetically initiating plans and ideas—hating to be caught in a maze of indecision.

You will expect your employees to be on time, arriving on the job fresh, exuberant, and ready for a day's work. They'll need to keep up with the fast pace you set, managing to run errands, polish up fragmented dictation, and catch you on the run when an answer to a question is needed.

You do not like to be disturbed when in conferences; however, you do tolerate and may even encourage being interrupted with questions of a constructive nature while discussing important plans or new projects. You appreciate honesty and are usually loyal to your employees. You may be blunt and to the point. Your staff shouldn't beat around the bush with you; they might find themselves beating a path right to the unemployment line. You become irritated with false gestures of sincerity and vague conversations that lead nowhere.

Number Two Employee

You're one of those workers who makes the boss look good. You're cooperative, tactful, mindful of the little details, and ready to do what you are told. You may not wish to be brought out into the limelight of recognition; quiet praise and an eventual raise in pay for your efforts is honor enough. All the glory doesn't matter, but money in the pocket does.

You are usually conscious of time, but there are

occasions when time seems to slip by and you arrive late. This doesn't happen often, though. You may decorate the office with a vase of flowers or grab a cup of coffee for your boss without being asked. If you are appreciated by your supervisor, you will return the gesture twofold. You are considered quiet, patient, and thorough in your position.

Even though not the type to boldly ask for an increase in pay, you'll still expect to be recognized for your loyalty and worth, and will desire to be rewarded accordingly. If an employer forgets to do this, he or she will have one upset and hurt employee. You don't like to bring up matters concerning pay but will stew and brood instead. You might even become a little more withdrawn and not perform to your best capacity; so your employer should check the calendar and your performance as he or she might have forgotten that it's time for your raise.

Number Two Employer

You are consistent. You will arrive around the same time every morning to begin the day (give or take a few exceptions). Not a pushy type of boss, you work patiently and would prefer an atmosphere surrounded by quiet and soothing music and not much confusion.

You are a mediator who will quietly listen to staff problems on and off the job and will not reprimand employees for being late on occasion. You are understanding of human error but perfecting in detail, and expect employees to be the same. Attention to little things is a requirement for all who work for you.

Number Three Employee

You're the one with the smile on your face who would rather be working near windows or where you can see the outdoors if you're in an office building. You can be quite sociable on the job and want to enjoy what you're doing. When you do something, it's handled with a flair of imagination; however, you can become side-tracked on occasion. If you've got more than one or two projects going at once, there are times you may not know which to begin or which to finish up first.

You will work overtime if necessary but want to choose the hours in which to stay late. You dress to suit the occasion and always have the appropriate outfit to match the job.

You will not want to work alone all the time but will do so on occasion. You fair quite well working in the public eye.

Number Three Employer

You can be an imaginative and humorous boss. You want to make the job a little easier. You believe in whistling while you work. When working, you will hope your staff keeps track of and remembers the things that you don't.

When illustrating assignments, you can add some color and humor to what you're explaining. You will define procedures as if telling a story. A dull or mundane task can seem like fun if you're the one who is delegating it.

You are an easygoing employer (unless you have a 4, 7, or 8 totaling your birth name). You'll want your staff to feel relaxed and happy on the job. You prefer a lighthearted atmosphere and will appreciate a joke or two all in fun; however, your workers should not make the mistake of thinking that you're a breeze to work for. You can catch an error quicker than the blink of an eye, and you'll expect corrections to be made. The hired help should make sure that when the amusement's over, they get down to brass tacks and be the kind of employees of which you will be proud.

Number Four Employee

See that person bent over the desk seemingly engulfed in serious thought? Quietly minding his own business, he takes the eraser, looks at the paper in front of him, and rubs out another tentative answer. You guessed it. It's you. You have the ability to take what was initiated by someone else on the job, polish off the rough edges, put it together in an orderly fashion, and present a fully completed and sound package. A 4 Birthpath architect I know wishes to do only working drawings where he's employed. Without a person like that, great designs would merely stay on paper, beautiful only in concept.

On the job, you're the one who's likely to pack a lunch rather than eat out too often. You prefer sticking to the work at hand and to a regular schedule. There are occasions when you'll cast your fate to the wind and splurge. It's at those times you may check out early for lunch and come back late. This action is usually forgiven, as it very rarely happens (unless you have a 3 or 5 totaling your birth name). You are considered reliable almost all of the time.

Number Four Employer

You expect your staff to follow directions to the letter. You may review what they've done, just to make sure. You worry inwardly that a project, task, phone conversation, or letter may not be carried out in just the right fashion. If you find fault with what is done, you will take over the matter yourself.

You'll take the time necessary to make decisions, not believing in jumping the gun. You are inclined to be practical and conscientious concerning plans and projects, even though you may appear a bit eccentric in some of your actions. If an applicant is looking to work for someone with common sense, you're the one who fits the bill. Those who appreciate a sense of discipline, organization, and routine will find it in you.

Number Five Employee

Talkative, quick on the trigger, and constantly moving describes your actions on the job. You're so charming, in fact, when you've made an error or mistake, you can rationalize the situation to the point that your boss finds himself or herself inclined to agree with you rather than reprimanding you. You are a clever individual who reacts quickly to any given situation.

Because of your dislike of routine, your love of travel, and your ability to be convincing and impressive, you are a natural in sales. You could walk into any office and make a cold call regarding typewriters, for example. Even though the organization has two typewriters, by the time you're done gliding along in conversation, they realize they're making room in the budget as well as in the office for a third typewriter. You can be hard to resist.

As an employee, you need enough space, somewhat of a free hand, and a variety of things to do. In your case, an idle mind for even a short period of time will cause you to spread your wings and fly from the nest of your present employment to bigger and better things.

Number Five Employer

You're quite changeable. It's very hard to tell what you'll do from one minute to the next. A restless nature and an active imagination are fitting, descriptive terms. Impatient with details and progressive in attitude, you are very adept at delegating responsibility. Doing so frees your time to think of ways to increase the company's assets.

You will want to find the quickest ways to get in touch with your staff at a moment's notice, and you'll want your employees to respond just as rapidly. You don't sit in the office regularly, either. One of your obvious characteristics is your distaste for being in the same place twice for too long a period.

You find it difficult to contain all your bubbly inner energy. If required to wait when you hadn't planned to, you may be found pacing back and forth. The mental flexibility you possess will ignite, on a weekly basis, new ways of improving procedures, schedules, and even the office decor. It's no wonder that the employee who works for you may walk away at the end of the day pulling his or her hair out. One thing's for certain: whoever works for you will never be bored.

Number Six Employee

You don't always win the prize for being the best salesperson on the job, unless you're working with products or services that you really enjoy. It's not because you can't do it, but rather because you believe in letting people make their own choices without your embellishing the sales pitch or putting on pressure. You are the type who will explain what you're selling then sit back and let the buyer decide. In other words, you're better at low-pitch rather than high-pressure.

You want to be compensated in direct proportion to the type of work being done. You like the security of a well-rounded benefit package and weekly salary, rather than straight commission (unless you have a 1, 3, or 5 totaling the birth name). Bonuses are definitely appreciated, provided they are added on to a consistent paycheck.

You're the type who will extend your helping hand over and above the call of duty. Whether it's making a cup of coffee, handling the boss's personal errands, or adding that extra touch of warm and caring interest toward fellow employees, you'll be there to extend your services when asked. You try to assist in repairing typewriters, fixing the Xerox machine, mending a jammed stapler. You are also the one who talks most about your home, family, pets, or general domestic concerns, with the exception of your personal relationships. As far as that subject is concerned, it's no one's business unless you decide you want to open up and discuss it.

Number Six Employer

The universal parent who keeps a watchful eye over all his or her employed children is what describes your attitude. It's not that you consider your workers child-like or immature; it's just that you have a way of wanting to take them under your wing and guide their steps carefully from behind the scenes. That is, of course, if you feel they deserve your guidance and respect. You are kind, considerate, and slow to burn when mistakes are made; however, your patience can be tried.

You will seem to forgive occasional errors, overlook those who stay out for lunch longer than usual, and may even disregard an employee forgetting to give you phone messages. Notice that I used the word *seem*. If they continue to slide along sloppily and to abuse your consideration, they will unexpectedly be slipping right out of a job.

You expect your staff to be one big, happy family, adjusting their schedules regularly to suit the needs at hand and getting along with everyone else.

You aren't necessarily snobbish or smug, but you do carry yourself with an air of confidence and superiority (especially if female). In fact, employees may feel as if they have to put their best foot forward as well as present a good image in dress around you.

You secretly would like your staff to ask your approval or come to you for advice, especially when the working relationship between employer and employee is a close one. One last thing—you would like your employees to keep their "cool" even while you're losing yours—and you do on occasion.

Number Seven Employee

You are quiet in nature (unless you have a 3, 5, or 8 totaling the birth name). You generally want to do a job in the best way possible; if you don't know something, you'll ask.

You want to know the reason behind an action. For example, if you're given a new task, you will ask questions about the project and how this task came into being. You have a way of getting to the root of an issue in seeking solutions.

Even though you are inquisitive, you are not the pestering type. In fact, with keen perception you often know what the answer is before you're told. Intuition is usually strong, unless you allow it to be clouded by false flattery. You love a compliment.

You can't handle too much pressure on a consistent basis, nor do you wish to. Besides, you already know the assignment needs attention, so you don't need anyone else pressuring you about it.

You'll need a quiet space in which to relax on a break. If you're in an atmosphere busy with phones and people, you'll try to find somewhere during your free time that is either outdoors or where taking off your shoes and resting offers enjoyment. Some of you bring books to work to read during lunch or on break.

Number Seven Employer

You are like the master wizard working diligently toward intellectual perfection. You are quite selective in how you want a job accomplished. You work well with graphs, charts, accounting, purchasing, or areas having to do with analysis.

You use quite a bit of intuition as well as intellect to solve problems. Staff members should be precise in typing memos, handling projects, or giving phone messages as far as you are concerned. They should also be prepared to advance their thinking abilities and be capable of looking into the future.

Many times you will leave decisions up to your employees. You don't like to play entertainer or babysitter. You will appreciate their decisiveness and foresight. If you think an employee is intellectually capable and analytically able, you will be more than confident and happy with him or her as an employee.

You prefer privacy when you work and do not appreciate interruptions that are not scheduled ahead of time. If you had your choice, there would probably be a Do Not Disturb sign posted on the door when important projects come up.

Generally, you are cordial and have a pleasing personality—once the ice is broken. But the employee will be the one who has to dissolve that wall of aloofness first. You don't want to be outshone. Maybe some of your employees do have more energy or more drive, but you control the steering. Because of your organized mind and cautious steps, you'll have more of the right answers in the final outcome. The staff has to get used to the unnerving fact that you are usually right.

Number Eight Employee

You are a mini-executive in your own right and can eventually do as good a job or better than the boss can (at least you think so). Many of you work in areas that deal with money or buying, or as supervisors and office managers.

When explaining tasks to other individuals in your peer group, you will show them the quickest possible method of completion, discussing what the end result should be like. You may not explain the details of the job at hand (unless 2s or 4s are predominant in the birth name). If they want specifics, they'll have to ask you. In relaying phone messages, you will touch upon the important points, not the inconsequentials. Therefore, you have a tendency to talk in tangents or fragmented sentences from time to time.

You are one of the first people to figure out company politics, the hierarchy, and who has the most say in the office, probably within the first week on the job. You can be a good judge of character.

Your senses are stimulated by being offered advancement that proves worthwhile and long-lasting. You're on the ball, so you will not stay with a company for too long (unless you're in a bind) that does not encourage promotion, recognition, and the chance to work up to an executive capacity.

Number Eight Employer

Wyatt Earp with dollar bills in his holster in place of a gun characterizes your image. The executive with a smile, a cool yet energetic disposition, and a genuine air of authority describes your nature. Having money and making it pleases you.

You don't put on a show for anyone—you are the show! You know how to delegate, demand, and demonstrate the control and leadership ingrained within you. You want to be "pro" all the way.

If the staff wants to play it smart and stay on your good side, they should impress tactfully, work within the budget, and employ a successful image (you are impressed with image). Parading their achievements like peacocks or playing coy little games to advance in rank will leave them out in the cold. You can be as sweet as sugar all the while you're planning to do some ousting because your feathers have been ruffled a bit too much.

You are adept at living by the law of the jungle in the business world, which amounts to survival of the fittest. Game playing is one of your specialties, and you can smell a phony a mile away. In fact, you may enjoy taking up the challenge.

You will advance an employee's position as well as his or her pay as quickly as possible if the person is helping to increase production, profits, and the company's image.

Small thoughts are not your style; so employees should think big (but not bigger than you do), value growth, and, above all, apply organizational efficiency and professionalism, if they want to be put on your promotion list.

Number Nine Employee

You don't mind tying up loose ends for others on the job, remembering to do what they might forget. You're a loyal employee who can adapt to any work situation for a lengthy period of time. If you are not situated in the right kind of job, you can begin to grumble. Believe me, when you've become irritated, moody, or upset, Scrooge never looked so good.

You are zealous when employed in something you like, taking up the banner and producing unbelievable results. You can take a project or position that is faltering and bring it back to life. If employed in public relations or sales, you have the uncanny ability of attracting money through service given to others—literally producing monetary results through the capacity of increasing customers. You possess a magnetic charisma similar to the golden touch.

A dreamer at heart, you can see a project or task in its most ideal state, not necessarily the way it is in reality. In the office, you try to remain as impersonally friendly as possible. You hate to get in the middle of an office dispute, so you'll be elusive even though it seems as if you're taking a stand.

You may have your employer wrapped around your little finger; however, this is not done intentionally or for selfish reasons. It's just the charm you possess. You do know how to play the game of politics to get what you want, but you won't employ such tactics unless absolutely necessary.

Number Nine Employer

You can be quite easygoing, give or take occasional jaunts of moodiness and quiet spells. Generally, you like to talk. You believe in socializing with your employees and are concerned about their general well-being on the job.

You are an authority figure who finishes projects that other people start and may be considered a jack-of-all-trades in your position. You are the one who is called upon to make those long-distance business trips.

Your field of expertise is in public relations, service, or in the creative industries. Another area in which you might shine would be investigation (criminal or research). Your sensitive perception and intuition helps costume you the modern-day Sherlock Holmes.

At times you prefer to be left alone for short periods during the day, but these moments are few and far between. Most often you will be dealing with people walking in and out of your office, group meetings, lectures, and consultations behind closed doors, not to mention phone calls coming in regularly. Even with all this action, you'll always leave word where you are or how you can be reached.

Number Eleven Employee

You'll attend to every detail on the job that is asked of you. You have your ups and downs in moods. You are an acutely aware individual who inwardly criticizes yourself more than anyone else ever could; so to remind you only once to correct an error or mistake is usually quite sufficient.

You seem to be a tiny bit flighty yet a sensitive creature who may be quiet and timid, speaking only when spoken to. Once a boss becomes more familiar, he will notice a drastic change. You then become more talkative (chitchatting), seemingly more outspoken, and not as flighty as first anticipated.

The making of quite a few friendly acquaintances is not uncommon when you're on the job. There are times you may not seem to notice someone in the office because you are so preoccupied or busy. Then, all of a sudden and out of nowhere, you will acknowledge that person's presence by remarking about a detail you've noticed regarding the person's hair, clothing, or something that caught your eye, and you begin to strike up a conversation.

You are considered to be ahead of your time, expressing futuristic ideas and brilliant brainstorms that may prove to be quite profitable to the boss who takes the time to listen. Having you as an employee could be a valuable and enjoyable experience—once the boss understands that you may not be of this world, but only live in it.

Number Eleven Employer

Loaded with energy and high-powered inventiveness, you can be a genius in your own right. The spark of exuberance lies quietly for one minute and in the next you'll explode zealously, darting here and there while implementing the inspirational ideas just received.

You need an employee who can help you keep the books. It's not that you lack ability in posting credits and debits, or assets and liabilities; you just don't have the time to be organized in your financial affairs (unless you have a 4 or 8 totaling the birth name).

You are adept at motivating your employees to produce results. You are the type who will offer incentive programs, bonuses, commissions, or words of praise and may even give your staff a choice of hours in which to work—provided it's within the workday schedule.

Just as with the number 2 employer, you appreciate the little things: tidying up the office, watering the plants, going out to lunch and bringing back a snack as a surprise, etc. All these seemingly minor details will not be forgotten in your book. You are a sensitive individual and are able to see both sides of an issue. You may not look as if you are paying attention all the time, but you're soaking up impressions like a sponge. Everything that goes on in your domain is carefully observed.

Number Twenty-Two Employee

Truth, honesty, and inner endurance characterize your nature on the job. You and the Rock of Gibraltar have one thing in common—immobility. When you've made up your mind to stick with it, that's exactly what you do.

You are often called upon to improve or expand projects or ideas. You are not necessarily the initiator at the office, but are the one whom the idea makers come to for practical advice. You could be the ambassador of your peers and can literally transform a small project into a complex operation.

You are inwardly sensitive, but your pride won't allow you to show it. Your integrity is real and is quite sincere. You may appear to be conservative and possibly even a little stuffy in the eyes of your peers, but this is not really the case.

The point is you are disciplined, outwardly calm, very practical, and often overinvolved in work. The emotions take a backseat. Consequently, you appear to be lacking in luster, imagination, or humor in the office. Because you have a tendency to overinvolve yourself, taking even a few minutes out of your schedule bothers you inwardly until the job is completed. That's why you will not ordinarily be one of the first ones to tell a joke (unless you have a 3 totaling the birth name). You'll probably be one of the last ones to hear it.

Once you've accomplished the task, the fun begins and you play hard. Whatever you're involved in, it's usually all the way.

Number Twenty-Two Employer

You can turn a small business into a large conglomerate or operate a smaller business in a big way, being the practical idealist you are.

You have a place for everything and everything has a place, even if you're the only one who knows where it is. If you reach for something in a familiar area and don't find it, it is comparable to watching the calm and conservative Dr. Jekyll turn into the angered and outraged Mr. Hyde. Your staff should be careful not to step on or bruise your ego. You hide much but forget little.

It's hard to get to know you; so employees shouldn't expect to become too familiar. There will be a side to your personality that they will never really know well, because you take time and practice caution before you advance into socializing with your staff.

You are selective when hiring employees. You expect the best and usually get it; if not, it's "There's the door . . ." However, you are protective of your personnel and can be very loyal once you've decided they're worth it. If an employee passes your scrutiny (which takes time), you will be a cherishing and devoted employer. Once you're happy with your staff, you will do everything possible to keep the workers happy, content, and, above all, secure.

Number Thirty-Three Employee

You are an excellent worker who is quite dependable, attracts customers, and can be relied upon not to betray a trust. You are extremely creative and, when given the right support from peers, will astound others with your imagination, zest, and ability to touch the hearts of the public. The catch is you need little reminders and a gentle push of confidence and backing every now and then. Once that motivation is present, almost nothing can stop you.

45

You are a practical artist on the job—congenial, helpful, and one who adds a homey personal touch to your business surroundings. No one should put it past you to pack a lunch for yourself and friends at the office or to bring in a box of doughnuts.

Your personal break time at work may consist of organizing social functions or making phone calls and running errands having to do with civic groups such as the Boy Scouts, Girl Scouts, or the PTA. Many of you are involved in physical fitness and spend your break time jogging, exercising, playing a game of raquetball, etc.

You can handle projects that include setting up banquets, large conference meetings, travel reservations, or even jobs that include advertising for the company. You'll perform these affairs with efficiency and expertise.

Number Thirty-Three Employer

You can be quite amazing in your approach to life. You believe in helping those less fortunate. You might hire the handicapped, teach apprentices, and counsel those employees who have personal problems. An excellent manager over your employees, you include the human elements of emotion and understanding. You will expect them to live by your rules in the office, adapting to your ideals and values, rather than switching your way of thinking to adapt to theirs.

You can be quite emotional and at times ramble in conversation, not stopping long enough to take a breath. You may want two copies of a letter instead of one or have more than one conversation going on at the same time. You like to expound upon ideas without reaching the point instantaneously. Others may, on occasion, have to read between the lines with you.

You are a unique individual who can see the scope of a situation from a commercial as well as humanitarian point of view. You're best suited to work for a universal and common cause that deals in the needs of people: medical or educational services, services that improve the physical appearance, domestic care, ambassadors, and counselors. You feel the weight of your position and carry more than your share of the responsibility.

3

Sex and the Single Number (& for Married People too!)

No need to explain this chapter; the title says it all. I do want to clarify that this section contains little nuances, personal preferences, and attitudes you have regarding your sexual nature; in other words, what you like and dislike.

Once again, look to your Birthpath number and/or your Name Number (look to Chapter 4 for numbers to names), then check below. Find out a little bit more about the way you operate, and realize that other individuals who read this chapter will now know how you conduct yourself. Too bad, not all matters are as private as you think.

Number One Birthpath

"Tally-ho and away we go" or "Wham bam, thank you ma'am/sir," is the spirit of your attitude and habits concerning sexual affairs. You are aggressive, impatient, and usually willing to try anything once. Sometimes, all it takes is an introduction or a little coaxing from your partner when venturing into a new sensation of physical pleasure.

Foreplay isn't quite as important as the real thing

for you; so, naturally, building up the slow crescendo does need some practice and patience. You need to realize that not every lover is ready to jump in the sack and go at it, so to speak. Once understood, you become very enthused yet caring and quite gentle in touch. You, as the initiator, can tease and arouse quickly to bring your lover to a state of pleasure that is ultimately fulfilling.

You don't like to be kept waiting in bed, either. If your lover teased you enough to get you there, he or she had better deliver and soon. You are a toucher also. The two of you can be walking around at a carnival and oops, your partner feels the quick movement of a hand brushing his or her backside. Your mate turns to you in amazement and finds you grinning from ear to ear. Quick Draw McGraw, that's what you're like, all right.

Number Two Birthpath

Sensitive and romantic, you will not appreciate being hurried along. In fact, you'd teach the number 1s a few tricks; namely, how to get the most pleasure by making it last longer.

You enjoy hugging, kissing, and caressing in the privacy of your love nest. You need that tender affection. This way, you are assured that you are cared for and appreciated. Most 2s, whether men or women, inwardly want their lover to be the initiator and aggressor in lovemaking.

The mood needs to be set for you. You, the idealist, are enchantingly swayed by candlelight, soft music, and a walk in the moonlight. You need to be complimented sincerely concerning your looks and told how much your partner would enjoy making love to you. Building you up verbally and touching you lightly is one of the sure ways to ignite the flame of love.

Number Three Birthpath

Your creative imagination will keep your mate forever hopping in your den of sexual pleasure. You can be a fun-loving individual. After a thrilling romp under the covers, you're the type who will suddenly throw a pillow at your lover, and then the playful battle begins.

You need to be given all the attention possible in bed and out. If not, you (no matter how old) can throw temper tantrums reminiscent of *The Taming of the Shrew*. Your mate shouldn't forget to allow you little games of cat and mouse. After the frivolity is over, you'll become sensitive and sensual as you take your partner to love's peak. It would be a party neither one of you would forget.

Number Four Birthpath

Sturdy, reliable, and steadfast in lovemaking, that's you. You really enjoy earthy, physical passion and don't think twice about roughhousing it a bit—but just a little. You will surprise your mate with how long you can last before reaching the peak of pleasure—talk about control! Now, this will only happen if you want it to. If not, a sexual encounter with you could last about five minutes and the fun's over.

I will admit, though, you aren't that excited about trying new things. You have a standard way of making love and one that works for you. How logical you are. Why fight what you know is a surefire method?! It'll take some persuading on the part of your lover to convince you to go against your common sense and "swing" a little. Also, I wouldn't be surprised if you have a regularly scheduled time of the day or week in which to make love. Sound dull? Not really. To you this schedule is a fail-safe method to ensure that lovemaking does occur regularly. Is there a method to your madness? You bet!

Number Five Birthpath

This is the number of the tactile senses. You like to smell, taste, and touch. During a physical exchange of love, you may use fruit-scented creams or oils that not only smell good but taste terrific. You are a flexible individual who uses variety and who can adapt to love-making at the spur of the moment (unless you have a 4 or 6 totaling the birth name).

You don't want to be crowded in bed and need allowances for varying techniques if needed, as long as you both agree it will bring mutual satisfaction. Because you can adjust your mind and emotions to suit the occasion, making love can happen anywhere, provided, of course, you have some privacy. You will not always desire to experience physical pleasure in a pretty meadow on a chilly morning (usually you're half asleep anyway, and it's cold). But you will, at times, think of different circumstances and ways to please your lover.

If encouraged to speak up, you will tell your lover what you like and don't like in regard to what physically pleases you. Finally, your mate needs to remember that you change your mind rapidly; so he or she will need to catch you quickly to reap the benefits of your love.

Number Six Birthpath

You can do with or without sex; a pity, really. You can be so picky about what a mate should or shouldn't do that the whole romantic aspect of letting it develop naturally is lost.

The trick here is that you must be emotionally close to your lover, who must meet the standards prescribed, before you will let loose and enjoy yourself in bed. There are occasions when some of you have been known to just lie there hoping time passes quickly so you can be done with it and do something else. This is extremely

51

rare, but it does happen when you feel you have to perform rather than want to.

However, when all is right, you will express the serenity and the beauty behind lovemaking. You'll nuzzle, cuddle, and take your time. To top it off, you will be ready for a lovely session of pleasure at a moment's notice, especially the 6 man. A 6 woman needs more time for primping, looking sexy, etc., before she'll enter the bedroom.

You will gently nurture your lover to full and complete satisfaction. You believe in keeping tempo, helping to match your mate's moods with his or her physical actions. Everything's in sync when you take over; you can be considered a truly compassionate lover.

Number Seven Birthpath

You need time to prepare yourself mentally for sexual pleasure. When too much is cluttered in the regions of your mind, you can't concentrate on the moment. Once these thoughts are straightened out, you are extremely delicate and sensitive with your lover.

You can be straitlaced regarding sexual affairs or you can go to extremes. Either you've had more than a few sexual encounters or have had none, remaining celibate for lengthy periods of time. On occasion, you have been known to talk more about sex than actually engage in the act.

You believe that sex itself is not as important as intellectual rapport with your lover. You figure that you can get it anywhere (sex that is), but having true mental compatibility is a rarity, so you search for that perfection. Consequently, you can be physically turned on to someone who demonstrates keen awareness and know-how. By itself, a pleasing appearance won't necessarily light your fire, but couple the good looks with signs of mental camaraderie, and you can create a blaze of loving concern for your mate.

Number Eight Birthpath

An 8 can stare a sexual hole right through someone. You are the type who can undress your lover in public, if you really want to, just with your eyes. Your partner shouldn't play the game back unless he or she is ready to accept the challenge. You could make your lover look like a fool if all he or she has on his or her mind is to tease.

You can be unusual in your lovemaking sessions. You and your mate will experience things you've never tried before but always under your control and sensitive guidance. You will usually never do anything that would cause your lover to be uncomfortable, bashful, or restricted, yet you do have a way of bringing your lover out of a shell. You have stamina and become quite energetic and verbal in your sexual expression of love.

This freeness that you share happens specifically when you are in love. An 8 who is a one-nighter will be extremely passionate, yet somehow remain a bit aloof once the physical release has been accomplished. In addition, you are private concerning your sexual affairs. When in love, you are very protective of your lover and believe that the beauty of the sexual act should remain in the bedroom. An 8 does not like audiences.

You are the type who may buy copies of *Playboy*, *Penthouse*, or *Playgirl*, keeping the magazines hidden in the bathroom or in a secluded area of the bedroom or den.

Number Nine Birthpath

You are both passionate and compassionate. You, like the numbers 2, 3, and 6, need to have the mood set. Not the type to always whisper in your lover's ear or send little physical messages that say you want to make love, you'll spin fine lines of magnetism that attract your mate into your web. It is not easy to put a finger on what exactly it is that made the catch secure.

Once under the covers, you're a chameleon who wants to be both assertive and submissive in the same lovemaking session. Foreplay to you might mean a wonderful massage, starting from your feet up to the neck and not missing a crevice in between those two points. Because you need to be in the mood, a delicate massage will very often help to set the pace.

You will also adapt to the style of your lover. You want to please your partner; so you can role-play (once feeling comfortable and secure) and create images that will ignite his or her sexual imagination to its peak. Your lover may not need to read *Playboy* or *Playgirl* if you are around. It should be remembered that you equate love with sex and emotions, and to get the best from you, your lover has to give it back.

Number Eleven Birthpath

You are tactful and very cooperative while engaged in love's physical delights; therefore, you will appreciate your lover's being the same way. Consideration is a prime prerequisite.

Your partner will have to be extremely attuned to your needs. Your hints are so slight, you may not recognize the difference between a kiss that says "I love you" and a kiss that says "Let's go to bed." Let's face it, even though seemingly extroverted at times, you are actually quite shy.

You have a highly sensitized body; so the slightest touch in just the right places could send you swaying back and forth. In some cases, the pleasure reaction is so strong, you could start at one side of the bed and end up at the other in just a matter of seconds. If your lover is planning a touch attack, he or she had better be prepared for a reaction. (For more information, check Birthpath number 2.)

Number Twenty-Two Birthpath

You can purr like a kitten or roar like a lion in the love nest, and only on occasion will you exaggerate a little about your prowess, in order to keep up your image. For the most part, it's only logical to you that "If it feels good, do it!"; just don't get carried away.

You know how to open your conscious self to the sexual side of your nature. Although a very intense individual, you have the calmness and patience to lie back and anticipate your next movement, secretly capturing every pulsating ripple of pleasure. Using good common sense, you will activate your desires one step at a time. Since you realize that all good things come in due time, that could take more than an hour or so.

You prefer "au naturel," including the natural scent of the body. Certain after-shaves or perfumes are pleasing to the senses, but to you there is nothing like the aroma of a clean body just bathed or showered. (For more information, check Birthpath number 4.)

Number Thirty-Three Birthpath

The thrill of chasing or being chased could be just as exciting as getting caught. You can play the love game rather effectively using verbal innuendos and subtle flirtations. There are moments when your eyes are bigger than your sexual appetite, biting off a little more than you can actually chew. When that happens, emotional confusion ensues and you may not want to be sexually involved at all! It's best for you to enchantingly flirt rather than deliver—it's safer that way.

You can be another one of those playful partners. Although you may not show your lover daily the small consideration of physical affection, the proof is in the pudding of sexual pleasure. That's when your lover will be assured how much you care. You are the type who appreciates a long and warm embrace.

Appearing somewhat high-strung at times, you need to be shown patience just the way you practice it. You have a tendency to expect your lover to know what pleases you, so it's best to talk to your lover openly, encouraging each other to speak up on sexual preferences. This could take time. Don't give up. If your lover plays your game long enough, he or she just might win the prize—sincere, honest, and open loving. (For more information, check Birthpath number 6.)

4

Your Name Is Not
Just A Name

△ The two most important tools you own are the Birthpath (total of the birth date), as we've already discussed, and the total of your name, which we will be covering in this chapter.

Dealing with my clients both locally and nationally, I've heard some of them say either that they like the name given at their birth or that they do not. Well, your name is not just a name, it's the total expression of your outward personality to the world at large. It is how you want to be seen on a continuing, regular basis and, in addition, describes what avenue or direction you should be following. This direction will aid in highlighting and polishing the tools of your inner nature (Birthpath). It's very important, therefore, to employ both the qualities of the birth name and the Birthpath for best success.

First, you'll need the complete name on your *birth certificate* in order to be accurate. Now that you have it, look to the scale that follows for the letters of the alphabet and the numbers that are assigned to those letters. For example, A is the first letter of the English alphabet, so it has the value of 1; Z is the twenty-sixth letter of the alphabet and, when reduced, has the value of 8 $(2 + 6 = 8)$, and so on.

```
1 2 3 4 5 6 7 8 9
A B C D E F G H I
J K L M N O P Q R
S T U V W X Y Z
```

To find the number that expresses your personality, you'll add together both the vowels of your birth name and the consonants and reduce that total to one number (with the exception of 11, 22, and 33).

Let's take an example:

```
HENRY   DAVID   THOREAU
8 5597  4 1494  2 869513  =  90 (9 + 0) =
9 Name
```

In short, the total of the name is like the overcoat for the real you that is covered up and protected from the wind and the rain of everyday living. It's the outer nature that cloaks our inner being (Birthpath) and tells us where and in what type of avenue we can place our natural talents.

Again, begin by using the full name as it appears on your birth certificate. This is the imprint, the stamp you were given, and it will tell the real story as well as describe you. Any other name you may be currently using is only a costume you're wearing over the real you. The birth name will always come through, either to enhance or hinder any nickname, career name, etc., you might be using.

With that in mind, let's get started. After you've added up your name at birth, find the number below that symbolizes and describes this outer expression.

Number One Name

Your personality expresses leadership and pioneering efforts, but be careful not to spurt flames of fiery enthusiasm unless you know you can make them last. You head projects, start new ventures, and can break the mold of tradition. On occasion you may want to jump new ladders before the old ones are taken down and may not last the duration.

Overall, you're the one who gets the ball rolling. You show independence, fortitude, and promote honesty—sometimes to the point of too much frankness or bluntness. Nonetheless, you'll call it like you see it.

Be involved with people who are doing original and innovative things. Your willingness to go where "angels fear to tread" may find you at the head of business or creative endeavors. Who knows, you may end up chairman of the board! Fields that allow you to move up the ladder are for you. Advance and don't be afraid to stand on your own two feet. Be strong, capable, and self-reliant. By doing so, you will enjoy the benefits that will be yours to claim.

Number Two Name

You can express gentle persuasiveness. Little do they know that behind the personality of tact, diplomacy, and the desire to please can lie the Rock of Gibraltar. Ideally portrayed, you're the one who mediates and arbitrates problems by bringing together opposing forces to mutual harmony.

You are a good listener—one who prefers to balance both sides of the issue before making a judgment. On occasion, you may have trouble being emphatic about an approach to a solution because you don't want to be wrong. It is also possible that you've covered both sides so well that you'd rather leave it up to the other person to make the final choice. Henry Kissinger, look out!

I will admit that at times you can be emotional if pushed to the limit; so those around you should understand that beneath the still waters can lie a whirlpool of turbulent feelings.

Partnership or team spirit is important, but do remember you don't have to rely on someone else in order to be successful. You might move up the ladder by working with groups or associations, or be involved with careers that attend to facts, history, or details. From the dramatic or design aspect, you'd benefit by working behind the scenes as a stage manager or writer. Some of you with a creative Birthpath number in conjunction with your 2 Name may be actors or actresses.

Number Three Name

The sunshine person, that's what you're here to express, even when the going gets tough. Creative opportunities and an optimistic outlook are what you have going for you; so don't hesitate to use them! Areas of entertainment that bring joy to others are a fine way to accomplish this task. Look at the name Billy Joel.

```
BILLY  JOEL
2 9 3 3 7  1 6 5 3  = 39(3 + 9) = 12 (1 + 2) = 3 Name
```

This is the name he uses for his singing career, and it benefits not only himself but all those with whom he comes in contact through his musical ability. You have a flair for the imagination and the arts; so go for it!

I'm not saying that all of you with 3 Names should be singers. What I am saying is to look down the sunnier side of the street and show others the way to get there. Also, mix with those individuals who know how to bounce back after serious setbacks. They'll teach you much. Other areas open to you deal with the mind and the gift of intuition, which could lead to studies in metaphysics, clairvoyance, etc.

Whatever you do, you're here to do it well and with optimism. You'll be popular, have love, and meet people. This is all possible if you smile, laugh your blues away, and get on with the tasks at hand.

Number Four Name

Your personality is what rocks and concrete are made of. You believe in order, system, and logic. You work hard and play hard. Set your sights toward being a manager, if you aren't one already, and an organizer for other people's ideas. Working consistently, one step at a time in a nine to five type of discipline pays off.

Backsliding into laziness will bring stumbling stones of frustration, lack of stability, and lack of accomplishment. Be careful to build from the ground up. On the other hand, don't overwork or worry, for that doesn't serve any useful purpose either and may cause your health to suffer by way of muscle aches and pains or exhaustion.

At times it may appear as if you're doing all the work and getting none of the credit. Be patient; your pat on the back will come. Avoid stubbornness or too fixed an attitude when others approach you with ideas or ways for doing things differently.

Work along lines that are practical and worthwhile. Some of your friends, for example, may be lawyers, political scientists, or construction engineers. In addition, 4 is one of the numbers that deals with property, and real estate may be suitable for you to pursue. Also, working with machinery (the mechanic) or agriculture might be beneficial, not to mention the health care services (orthodontist, dentist, hospital work, etc.).

You are the foundation in which others can plant their roots and be secure in the knowledge that storms will not upheave what they've accumulated, if they put their trust in you.

Number Five Name

Progress is the key word here. Flexibility and adaptability are the keynotes of your personality. Opportunities lie in your ability to communicate effectively and "sell" what you have to offer, both with your mind and with your mouth. You can sell a freezer to an Eskimo or an arrowhead to an Indian, all in a matter of moments.

You're not the type of personality who likes to be stuck in a routine. You want to know what's going on, and you work on any angle that allows you to accomplish this goal. The routine endeavors will not appeal to you. You want to be free of restrictions or limitations.

You can switch subjects quickly and project a tremendous amount of magnetic charisma. Flash—you are noticed! You have the capacity to impress others with your knowledge, but don't overdo it or sell a bill of goods simply because you want others to see your point of view. That would endanger your bargaining power and your credibility. In other words, don't give the wrong impression at any time. There is responsibility attached to your sense of freedom and variety, and you are required to carry your message in the right way.

You can be a natural investigator because of your curiosity; therefore, areas dealing with the law may be suitable. Advertising, promotions, or trades involved with communication are also open to you. You may be drawn to journalism or song and jingle writing.

Open doors to people who are doing progressive things in the world. Your life will pave the way for very interesting and unique encounters. Use your charisma, intelligence, and freedom of movement to make this world a better place in which to live.

Number Six Name

Service to your family and community seems paramount in your eyes. You are loyal to your immediate kin and can be like a protective parent over your husband, wife, children, and close friends.

You give an awful lot to your emotional ties, but underneath, you expect much in return. You'll need to loosen the strings that bind your love with expectations or possessiveness, so that you don't put people on pedestals where they don't belong. When loved ones fall from the stage of emotional perfection, the image you've created shatters into pieces of broken ideals and sentiment. Nine times out of ten, they weren't aware of the expectations you placed on them.

You're an excellent listener to the needy and can really be considered the true humanitarian. Be sure you don't allow yourself to go down with the ship in attempts that will prove futile just to save someone from peril.

You may be somewhat of a perfectionist and enjoy the satisfaction of doing your job well, but you also expect proper payment for your efforts, i.e., to be respected and appreciated for the time, energy, compassion, and knowledge you possess. You have earning capacity and can attract a sizable amount of money on the job, but remember, your reward will equal your responsibility.

Music may be an area of interest, and many 6s I know have excellent voices. Another field of interest is food, for example, gourmet cooking, taste testing, or researching for new recipes. You may also think about spending some time working with groups in your community who are trying to improve their surroundings on a social, political, economic, or environmental level. The 6 is one of the numbers for healing and the healing services (hospitals, medicine, health insurance, etc.) or for work in a mental/emotional setting (sociology, psychology). All these fields could be beneficial in the enhancement of your caring nature.

Number Seven Name

Cool and collected, this number expresses analyzation and the student thinker. A 7 asks "why" instead of "what." You're the type who prefers little noise and confusion when concentrating.

Sometimes experiences will draw and test your ability to separate illusion from reality and teach you that the grass is not always greener on the other side of the fence.

Technically- and analytically-oriented as you are, the lines open to you deal with the sciences, including the study of marine life or navigation. On the other hand, other specialties could incorporate philosophies on the university level. Some of my 7 Name clients are excellent research writers. Finally, health foods and/or vitamins prove to be rewarding fields of expression.

You will find that some of your successes will be realized through unusual or nonordinary lines of endeavor. For example, a client of mine who has a 7 Name is an architect. He has broadened his career by incorporating ideas and designs that are considered unusual or advanced (i.e., solar energy) long before their application and use were considered feasible.

This number carries a subtle mystique. People seem to want to find out more about you because of your kind yet somewhat mysterious personality. You are not one to allow your life to become an open book to just anybody, and although you may ask questions of others, you're not as apt to answer many personal questions asked of you.

Whether it be playing the part of the chameleon or advancing highly skilled specialties, whatever you attempt will be done in the best way possible, leaving no stone unturned until you have the proper answers.

Number Eight Name

Move over Rockefeller, leave a space in history for this name too. You have a very strong outward personality, one that can take the punches as well as give them. Like the number 1 Name, this personality thrives on competition and strives for making something of itself. The difference is once you get there, you have no intention of leaving the post to hop a freight train for the next pioneering challenge. You play for keeps.

This personality is controlling and influential. It very rarely melts from the heat of pressure, although there are some exceptions. Others along the road of life will look to you as the delegator and organizer of larger projects or plans and as a personal problem solver of their dilemmas. You're the expresser of the "executive in charge," whether in personal or business affairs. Unlike the number 1 Name, who has ego and pride in abundance that is expressed openly, the 8 Name leaves those attributes lurking in the shadows. Then, when needed, the 8 calls upon its mastery slowly, like tiny tremors that give warning of an earthquake about to unfold, once beckoned to "do its thing."

You strive for balance between ethics and material gains and accomplishments. There are times when doing something for the satisfaction of fulfillment is better than the monetary results alone. You will be put to the test. What do you value most? You will continually weigh your spiritual and material beliefs, producing both ethics and stamina, while setting your sights to larger aspirations. Do you strive to be at the head? You do, and very often reach that epitome of success. Understand, it may take repeated efforts to get there, and remember, delegate graciously when setting your plans into motion.

Property matters, buildings, or their supervision are some areas to pursue. Other avenues would include metaphysics; or working with churches, hospitals, universities; supervisory capacities; or directing projects. Your precision and ability to see the whole picture accurately and quickly may attract you to fields of finance where you can employ your knowledge of money matters. Marketing, banking, legal matters, such as trust funds, etc., may all fall under this jurisdiction. You're not one to vacillate about anything or to think in small pictures. No, this number is Panavision; so go for it.

Number Nine Name

Understanding, compassion, and impersonal love for the many are what you're here to express, not to mention being a catalytic vehicle for others' experiences and growth. Many times you'll be called upon to complete what someone else has started. Sounds like a big job, doesn't it? Don't worry, you can handle it. You really can be blessed with many friends and many opportunities in life. You must stand for your ideals and make your place in the world more beautiful and generous. The arts, the colorful, philanthropy, research, and the aesthetic are some of the parts that fit into the "cog" of the wheel of your expression.

Perfect the art of forgiveness and the ability to view the broad spectrum, and you will be gratified with returns in abundance. Those of my clients who express the number 9 outward personality have done just that and have been surprised and grateful at the rewards that came bouncing back.

Anything to do with law might be suited to you as well. In fact, add up the word *law* and see what number it totals.

LAW
3 1 5 = 9

Seek employment where the people are important. This might include employment counseling or areas dealing with intangible services offered to the public to

66

help people improve themselves. In addition, some 9 Names choose the creative fields. Traveling on the road of your career may highlight dramatic or musical talent. At some point in the life of a 9 personality, interest in music, acting, or even purchasing many record albums or tapes becomes important, if only for a short time.

The opportunities can be quite limitless for a 9 Name as it is the symbol for the all-encompassing. If the natural talents of your Birthpath number are in conjunction and/or complementary, you can do almost anything successfully. The trick lies in your ability to see the picture as a whole in its most ideal state, while still keeping your feet firmly planted on the ground so as not to dream your life away.

Go ahead, take on a job that will allow you to expand your horizons with different peoples and places to travel to from time to time. You'll be glad you chose a career like that. So will everyone else!

Number Eleven Name

You philosophize and ignite. There's electricity attached to your outward personality. Like a double-edged blade, you have the choice to illuminate in the limelight or to inspire from behind the scenes.

This name number doesn't always revel in telling others what to do but can have such a way with words that the person listening won't mind giving up command to your final decision. Yet inwardly, you feel that you don't want to take the responsibility for being wrong in your judgments. On the one hand, you will hesitate; on the other hand, you can clearly see both sides of an issue; so you won't give bad choices in the first place. It then becomes a toss-up for those who come to seek advice. In the end they'll leave not with one answer but at least two.

Although full of energy, get-up-and-go, and outward confidence, there's a part of you that has trouble handling the center of attention. You want that spotlight, but when it's there for the taking, you cover your charming bashfulness as best you can. How? Sometimes by overcompensation.

The areas of design, philosophy, the stage, or historical facts and figures may be part of the repertoire from which you choose. For those of you quieter 11s who would rather inspire from behind-the-scenes, banking, counseling, or possibly writing would be appropriate. In addition, specialized fields of psychology are open. Some of you are also attracted to electricity or water and choose these areas. Most of you can be very advanced thinkers in your own right; so keep open the channel of your inventiveness. Whatever you do, carry the torch of illumination always at your side. You are the idea person who will reap the bountiful pleasures that come with enlightening others. You believe in sharing.

Number Twenty-Two Name

When you do something, you want to do it right. That's all there is to it. Some people may think you are a bit slow in the decision-making process. That is so far from the truth, it's pitiful. When you make a decision, it's accurate; therefore you'll plan, organize, and make sure all the bases are covered before you go ahead and slide for home plate.

Let them think what they want. When they've jumped the gun and come out losers, they will come, with admiration, to you for advice, because you've built a life of security, while others have been left swimming in a whirlpool of "here today and gone tomorrow."

Family and foundation are important, but in-laws, relatives, or being caught in a rut can take up much of your time if you allow yourself to be bound and restricted by an out of proportion sense of duty, tradition, or security. You're as loyal as the day is long, but sometimes you'll need to know how to bend like a willow instead of stand like an oak. In a hurricane, an oak tree can become uprooted, but a willow very rarely does.

You're just as familiar with thinking and doing big things as anyone else. Career drives and aspirations may be looked upon as if they are huge conglomerate goals. You usually get the results you're looking for through perseverance, stamina, and foresight—all of which you regularly express like second nature. Far be it from you to stop the wheel of progress, especially when it's moving in your direction. Why just build a city? Make it a state!

This outward personality can represent a fascination with gadgets or how to fix things. Areas open to you could be in land or landscaping, instrumentation, minerals, oil, and the like. Others of you may make a career out of being the rock of their own business.

Interestingly, the wonderful world of fantasy to see in the United States is Disneyland. Take a look at its numbers.

```
   9     5 7  1       = 22/4   Vowel
D I S N E Y L A N D
   4   1 5     3  5 4 = 22/4   Consonant
                       44/8   Name
```

Both Vowels (desire) and Consonants (the facade) express bigness (22/4). (More about Vowels and Consonants later.) It is a mastery of fantasy—not to mention a large pocketbook (8 Name).

You have the ability to make your dreams come true and put them into reality, not just to desire, but to do. Medical technology fields would be another avenue to pursue. Many 22s work with their hands as well as with their minds. The arts—either playing or writing, music, photography, and the like can be suitable endeavors. In these areas, a 22 has not only the talent to use brainpower but the manual dexterity as well.

Yours is a personality that builds a foundation for dreams to come true. Don't let this talent lie dormant.

Bring it forth, and behold the structures you'll create for yourself and others.

Number Thirty-Three Name

Other people seem to respect you instantaneously. There is a quiet "knowing" that permeates your personality. You speak and individuals will automatically listen. You can be loved by many for the cosmic caring you express.

You have a controlled dynamism, like keeping nuclear energy behind lock and key, but the power is nonetheless perceived. In fact, you can radiate so much that others may not even notice anything else about you, such as what type of after-shave or perfume you're wearing.

Either the concern for material aspects and getting ahead is extremely important or you'll recognize that monetary success and straining for it is not as necessary as others think. The path will be provided through inner faith and the understanding of the "wheel" of the universe.

You are here to serve through the example you set for others. The fields of sociology, social and welfare work, or politics would be suitable. In addition, delving into metaphysics to discover hidden truths would be rewarding. Also, there may be interest in working with the land and maintaining its beauty or making yourself known in the field of medicine.

5

You Look Like You've Got It All Together

▲ You've heard that saying "Don't judge a book by its cover." Well, the cover of that book is the façade, and it is arrived at by the *total of the consonants* in the name at birth. You will find out more about that in this chapter.

The total of the consonants, sometimes referred to as the Impression number, reveals to others what you seem to be like at first glance, before they get to know the real you. For example, I have a client who is very bouncy, likes to talk, and always seems to have a smile on her face. At first glance, others may not take her seriously or might think she's a bit flighty. Once people get to know her, they realize how much depth, perception, and seriousness she possesses. What people discern at first glance is the impression she gives based on the consonants of the birth name. These total 3, which epitomizes those qualities I have just described.

Using the chart at the beginning of Chapter 4, take the consonants of your birth name, add up the prime digits of the consonants, and reduce to a single digit. The total symbolizes the impression you give at first glance.

Karen J. David

Here's an example of the late, once-famous comedian Jimmy Durante:

```
J A M E S   F R A N C I S   D U R A N T E
1 4 1 69  53 1 4 9  5 2   =
50 / 5 + 0 = 5   5 Consonant
```

Here was a man of charisma who touched the universal chords of the public. Jimmy Durante seemed to give the impression of the freedom-loving type of individual who could cast his fate to the wind. He spoke his mind, both convincingly and charmingly. Naturally, his 5-like impression became the style imprinted on the minds of his viewing audience for years.

Add the consonants in your birthname, and find that explanation of your number Consonant listed below.

Number One Consonant

At first glance, you don't appear to be too talkative. Rather, you possess a distinct sense of authority and leadership. You seem to have quite a bit of nervous energy, which doesn't necessarily show in outward gestures, but rather radiates from within you.

You can seem to be a very smooth operator and look quite tall because of the way you carry yourself, even if you're only five feet in stature. The Statue of Liberty could look small in comparison to the image you wish to present to the public upon first meeting! After about twenty minutes, the impression of "look up to me" dissipates and the easygoing manner sheds forth that really is yours to claim (depending on your Birthpath and the total of your birth name).

This number also indicates you are a person whose dress will be a little bit more tailored. Even if the style marks the latest fashion, you don't want to be bogged down with layer upon layer of clothing.

Number Two Consonant

The facade you carry appears quiet, somewhat reticent, and composed. Dressing in pastel colors and soft fabrics marks the gentleness you convey upon a first meeting. You seem to be a good listener; although at times you may appear reluctant to respond because of an acute case of shyness. That is, of course, until you're known better. Once the ice is broken, you join in the conversation.

Others may get the feeling that you need protection from the cold, cruel world, because of the delicate nature they think they're perceiving. When the veil lifts, however, these new acquaintances might find out that you're more than capable. That's what they get for judging the book by its cover!

Number Three Consonant

Bouncy, lighthearted, and smiling characterize the qualities others see in you on initial contact. They may even think you're a person who never becomes depressed, worried, or self-conscious. Little do they know the real truth, right?

You're fashionable and carry an air of imagination in your clothing. People believe you to be the life of the party, and you are invited to quite a few social events. Their basic impression of you is one of friendliness. When the twinkle in your eyes starts to glimmer and that smile beams with brightness, it's difficult for anyone to remain uncomfortable in your presence.

Number Four Consonant

My goodness, what a solid image you put forth to the public! You're observed as a stable, somewhat conservative, and disciplined sort of individual who gives the impression of being secure and calm.

The image presented is subtle and that of one possessing a fixed attitude and an intent purpose shown by listening to what others have to say. At times, you seem to be the one that others come to for advice on mechanics, lawn and gardening, and household repairs (even though you may not be interested in those things at all!).

You may like tailored styles that are all-purpose and functional, with colors ranging from robust browns to light beiges or natural. You're not one to demonstrate flashiness on first meeting. You'd rather wait until you're known better before the garments that are glittery, unique, and quite out of the ordinary are hauled out of the closet.

Number Five Consonant

Others see you as the type who could easily become bored. You seem to stay in one place for only short intervals, mixing and mingling. Then, packing up yourself and your goods, you travel to the next adventure. A 5 represents a progressive individual who can be ahead of his or her time.

Initially, your peer group will observe you asking questions, giving opinions, and generally keeping pace with the action. Others may see you as being not too interested, because you have a tendency to get to the point of an issue rather quickly and charmingly just to satisfy your own curiosity. You are not the meddlesome type—you only appear to be at times.

Sexual magnetism is not uncommon with a 5 Consonant. You seem to radiate charisma, and consequently, the opposite sex may be attracted to you first. I wonder if that's how Don Juan got started?! Your style of dress may be trendy but is not ostentatious. You will always put your best foot forward in physical appearance—right down to the fingernails, which usually look clean, polished, and manicured.

Number Six Consonant

The image you project is one of being the cosmic parent and/or counselor. You seem to be the one that most people would want to talk to about their problems and from whom they would receive a comforting and quiet trust. Have you ever thought of putting out a sign that says "Florence Nightingale Resides Here" or "The Doctor Is In"?!

You appear congenial and kind but do not want others to force their opinions on you. The qualities of warmth and sincerity are part of your makeup, but others seems to know when to put the brakes on.

Dressing up in style is either very important to you or may not be important at all. When choosing your wardrobe, you may appear to be sophisticated or down to earth, depending on your mood.

Number Seven Consonant

You appear to be reserved at a business or social gathering until the ice is broken, then you feel more secure in the situation. The impression you may give is that of a person who has more questions than answers. You and the statue of "The Thinker" have things in common—the ultimate picture of analyzation.

Unlike the 5 Consonant number, you will satisfy your mind by picking apart questions and finding out the whys in conversation. You seem refined, dignified, and can carry an air of illusion and mystery; you have an almost untouchable quality. Others are attracted to your quiet sense of chivalrous intrigue.

Unless you're feeling out of sorts, the wardrobe you choose looks as if it had just been bought, taken off the hanger, and put on by you. The style of clothing may vary, but the image projected is usually fresh and appears neatly put together.

Number Eight Consonant

You seem to be the big thinker and sometimes the big talker as well. An 8 Consonant hints at saying and doing things on a large scale (even though it may not really be like you at all!).

Prosperity marks the image you first project. With this quality you can be capable of demonstrating to others that you're the president or director of a large company. You can even give the impression that you are extremely wealthy—a distant cousin of the city's richest individual.

Your peer group will view you as efficient, organized, and usually very well-tailored. You appear to be one who is impressed with impressions, even if you are not. Somewhat secretive at first, it is not easy to be open about your own personal or private beliefs, but you may enjoy trying to find out how other people tick. Some 8 Consonants have been known to tease, challenge, and sometimes unintentionally embarrass another person on their point of view. But this is very rarely done to hurt or cause trouble, rather it is a way of creating spark and liveliness in conversations; you and the 8 Birthpath have that in common. You seem to give the impression of having it all together both personally and professionally.

Number Nine Consonant

At first glance, you appear impressionable and generous in thought and action. When the veil lifts though, you may really be a little more economical than you first seemed. You project an enchantingly magnetic quality that draws people to your kindness and easygoing manner.

Your initial image is cosmopolitan and, in fact, worldly. You are perceived as a man or woman of wide experience and broad outlook, yet you may not have traveled much, let alone be acquainted with worldly encounters. Nonetheless, this is what can be pictured by others. You look to be the type who can adapt nicely to any environment, situation, or group of people.

Your wardrobe appears classical yet artistic. Colors chosen by you seem to be subtle and sometimes darker in shade: dark brown, black, mauve, blue, etc.

Number Eleven Consonant

Who is that dynamic person that just walked into the room? That's what someone else might be asking about you. The impression here is electric and vital, with sparks of energy and visionary capabilities. At least that's the way you appear at first glance and when you choose to turn on the charm! With you there is the choice either to radiate with exuberance or to quietly observe with reticence. To others, you seem to be a stimulating individual who can demonstrate seriousness or liven up conversations with airy and light discussions.

The colors you like are not as soft looking and pastel as your counterpart, number 2 Consonant. Rather, they shiver with vibrancy. Smooth materials, however, seem to be a must! (For more information, check number 2 Consonant.)

Number Twenty-Two Consonant

You, like the number 8 Consonant, can look quite wealthy—even if you're broke! There seems to be a picture of perfection and expertise that surrounds your appearance as you walk into a room.

Your clothing is neat and may look expensive, as appearance means much to your success in life. Wardrobe is chosen carefully; you select styles that are simple yet well put together.

Others view you as emotionally controlled—cooperative, yet practicing restraint. In reality this may not be the case. You could actually be a jolly joker who is carefree, expressive, and inclined to talk one's ear off. Nonetheless, the image first perceived can be likened to a generous, kind, but professionally conservative individual. (For more information, check number 4 Consonant.)

Number Thirty-Three Consonant

You seem to be quite talkative and congenial. It may not be hard for other people to make you smile or laugh. However, you also seem to be attracted to more than one philosophy, article of clothing, or more than one lover. You give the impression at times that you can't seem to make up your mind. In addition, your peer group may take you for an animal lover, although the thought of owning a pet may never be on your list of priorities.

Your wardrobe is bright and very stylish. At first appearance you could be considered one of the In Crowd. You can be viewed by some as high-strung or going to extremes when things don't happen the way you think they should. In all, the image here is one of being dependable, trustworthy, pleasantly charming, and humane. (For more information, check number 6 Consonant.)

6

What Motivates You?

O You, like all of us, are probably very interested in what makes people tick. We all have, to some degree or another, a curiosity about ourselves and others. What's that driving force behind the actions or the urges that push one's goals and aspirations from behind the scenes?

The number that can reveal this motivational tendency is found through the vowels of the birth name. The total of the vowels in the name is a very important number to look at, for those qualities represented will not be obvious to the naked eye unless you are really in close contact with the individual. It is, however, the underlying motivation for experiences and actions.

As another point of interest, the total of the vowels is one of the very important numbers to scrutinize and understand when trying to find how compatible you are with someone else.

To find out what motivates you, add the prime digits of the vowels of your name and reduce that number to a single digit. Find the numerical value attached to each vowel by referring to the chart at the beginning of Chapter 4.

For example:

6   5   1   9   = 21 / 2 + 1 =
                                 <u>3</u> Vowel

J O H N   E D W A R D   S M I T H

In the case of the letter Y, consider it a vowel when it is the only vowel sound in the name or when it takes on the sound of the vowel preceeding it (for example: Mary, Stacey, or Lynn).

Below is a description of each of the numbers and what they indicate in the vowel position.

Number One Vowel

You like to think you are Number One, the top dog, in both personal and business life. You desire to be the king or queen of your own castle, knowing that others respect your opinions and decisions.

There is a hidden drive to stand out in a crowd and to be accepted for your originality and fearless way of handling pressure. You're motivated by a sense of honesty and loyalty. The desire to stand on your own two feet and be self-reliant carries you through the rough spots on the road of life. Success will be yours if you practice determination, meet your challenges, and accept new directions as you travel to your destination.

Number Two Vowel

You wish you could always keep your waters calm and free from storms. Turbulent arguing, which upsets the placid motion of your personality, will urge you to fight to keep the peace.

The motivation here is for partnership and team spirit. Consequently, you desire appreciation and support when attempting new ventures, not necessarily wanting to be on your own even though you may appear to others to be the epitome of independence.

You're inclined toward the detailed; so the little things are important, even if you don't say so. You're

80

motivated by the romantic and sensitized by your own hidden idealism. Yours is the desire for a peaceful existence, full of love and cooperation.

Number Three Vowel

You secretly would like to be the center of attention and the life of the party. Motivated by imagination, you color your actions with fantasy and innocence, looking at others with wide-eyed wonder and amusement. You want to laugh, be optimistic, and claim recognition for some of your hidden creativity. You are motivated by sociability.

Friends, brothers, and sisters are important. You wish to get in touch more often. Also, you can adore little children, admiring the way they experience life. If you can bring a smile to someone else, it will make your day. At times, you may become gloomy or somewhat pessimistic if your admiration for another is not returned. How dare they not give you the applause you've so rightfully earned! Your motto should be "Laugh, and the world laughs with you; cry, and you cry alone."

You, the lover of love, wishing to spread it around, bring joy and optimistic seeds of experience through your creativity and imagination. You should not let those things go unnoticed.

Number Four Vowel

If you had your choice, you'd make sure everyone was just as practical, hardworking, and full of common sense as you are. Abstract principles aren't usually your strong suit. Putting it plainly, you're not motivated to push ahead by flowery speeches, theoretical notions, or fanciful gestures. You're influenced by concrete examples and discussions that lead to worthwhile results.

You long for stability and loyalty in love, choosing sensibly to express the devotion that is felt. You show your affections in very practical ways, like making sure your loved ones wear warm coats in the winter, stressing the importance of vitamins, getting to sleep at a decent hour, etc.

There is a hidden need to strive to be a manager of your own life and career. In addition, you may secretly want to be close to nature or to engage in a mechanical or physical hobby (i.e., plumbing, gardening, bowling, hiking). In short, you desire to represent the earthly things in life.

Number Five Vowel

You're like the "gypsy" at heart, desiring to move freely without restriction. You're motivated by curiosity, variety, and flexibility. The desire here is to do interesting things, meet interesting people, and visit interesting places. There is a hidden urge to be athletic, leaping tall buildings in a single bound. You wish never to fall into the trap of routine on the mental, physical, or emotional level.

The incentive for loving stems from friendship first. Your lover should be a companion and friend, one whom you can bounce ideas off of and say what you feel without having to walk on the eggshells of carefully worded phrases. Freedom in devotion minus possessiveness is what you search for in a lasting relationship.

You wish to share the knowledge you've acquired through experience. You'd make an excellent lecturer, for you can add the human element and those things that are common to all. By being adaptable and sharing what you know, others may be pointed in the direction of genuine progress.

Number Six Vowel

The parental side of you worries about your loved ones doing the right thing. This is especially so if you have children. Like the birds of the wild, you will recognize somewhat reluctantly that there comes the moment of departure. Even after your young have left home to fly away and build nests of their own, your subconscious cloak of patronage may still exist from a distance while you hover and wait to be there when needed.

Overall, you desire the best that life has to offer for yourself and those you love. This includes all the comforts of living, a trim and warmly decorated home, a harmonious environment, and a haven of family love and respect.

Number Seven Vowel

When was the last time you didn't want to analyze or rationalize a situation? Your desire is to seek out and find solutions through mental pursuits, in which you can become quite clinical or technical, leaving no stone unturned in the process. Questioning everything is how you prove things for yourself. You, like the number 6, hope for perfection. In your case, however, it's from an intellectual point of view, not necessarily from an emotional one.

Although gentle, caring, and extremely romantic in your desires, you'd still rather not get hung up on the emotional end of relationships if it can be helped. You'd rather have a lover you can talk intelligently with and who will admire your subtle, sometimes dry, witty sense of humor. You desire to be nice to everyone by displaying a quiet and chivalrous charm. Overall, you are actually very selective in choosing those people you call your friends. To you, what is illusion can be reality, and what appears to be reality is only an illusion. You try your best to discriminate between the two.

Number Eight Vowel

You feel an intense desire to be the executive authority who organizes and efficiently manages the affairs of others. Ambition is one of the strongest motivators. Those who seek your guidance and support will be quite pleased with the help you give. You're straightforward in your approach to solving difficulties and do so quickly. One thing is for sure—you don't think small, not by a long shot. However, in your exuberance, try not to overestimate your ability or anyone else's qualifications, for life will run much more smoothly that way.

In close personal relationships, you are passionate and deeply loyal. On occasion, the executive in you pushes too hard or causes you to treat your romances as you would a business. Though you might occasionally appear to be unemotional with those you love, you're nonetheless motivated by a strong sense of loyalty and devotion.

You seem to have your own thoughts regarding spiritual law and can be somewhat philosophically inclined, probing the higher forces and laws of discipline and balance. When carried to extremes, you could be a little superstitious. Overall, you do strive for balance between the spiritual and material aspects of life, and incorporate a sense of fairness and ethics in all your commercial undertakings.

Number Nine Vowel

A dreamer of the impossible dream, you inwardly perceive the world as it ought to be, not necessarily as it really is. You, like the number 6, desire to be of service. You are glad to be of assistance as long as you know those in need will then begin helping themselves.

You desire to be the perfect lover and companion. You are motivated by people and do not wish to be held back by a mate who thwarts your desire for experiencing public contact. You also dislike crudeness or a lack of appreciation. If not objective in love, emotions may blind your choice of a suitable partner.

The deeply embedded emotions you feel will sometimes overtake your motivations. At those times, in a striving for self, a battle will occur between your impersonal nature and your personal ambitions, and your ability to see the whole picture will fly right out the window.

Your urge is to be a world traveler and teacher. Enjoyment and satisfaction are gained when you strive toward universal understanding, tolerance, and charity. In you lies the desire for total harmony, where all walks of life can get along happily.

Number Eleven Vowel

You are motivated by an air of zealousness, wanting to charge up your being with inventive thoughts and actions. You wish to manifest all your ideas and hopes into reality and believe in expanding other people's awareness; you trigger their hopes through faith and enlightenment. You are a lover of the arts and things of beauty. You appreciate contacting people who stimulate your thought processes.

You are emotionally sensitive, and the poetry of love whisks you away with endearing gestures and soft romantic expressions, reminiscent of knights of old and fair maidens who promise their all.

The word *fight* is one you wish struck from your vocabulary and from the actions of those you love. You desire to mingle in peaceful, flowing unions; so there are times when you back down from arguments to keep the peace. A 2 in this position can also be a soft-spoken person who carries a big stick!

You're motivated by a sense of subtlety and gifted persuasion, recognizing the value of diplomacy to instigate results rather than pushing or using brute force. You can be a mystic and a mentor rolled into one.

Number Twenty-Two Vowel

You desire to be the Master Builder of plans and ideas. You wish you could innovate more productive and practical ways to improve mankind, like building safer highways, constructing a more effective means of communication between people, or organizing a better method of economizing to reduce waste. "Haste makes waste" is one of your mottoes.

You desire to be the rock upon which others can lean. You'd like to give and receive strength, stability, and security through the friendships and loves of your life. And please don't allow someone else to hurry you. You tend to grow impatient with impatience itself. Admiration and respect take time to develop; better to be steady and build a solid situation than to walk upon the shaky ground of uncertain, flash-in-the-pan exchanges.

Once you have mastered yourself and your desires, you begin to recognize that anything is possible. No feat is too large to tackle and systematize. You think of yourself as the grand schemer of large undertakings that bring results to the masses. With minds like yours around, one can understand how such things as pyramids came into being!

Number Thirty-Three Vowel

Care and consideration drive you along with the high principles and ideals you possess. You can sense goodness where others see none, for you innately can extract and explain a person's inner being.

Others may find it hard at times to comprehend the breadth of the seemingly cosmic understanding you possess. On occasion, you'll find yourself having to simplify things so they can be perceived and learned.

Through your encouraging influences, you can be like the Master Teacher.

In certain instances, you may desire to have your own set of double standards, particularly with those you love, i.e., "Don't do as I do; do as I say." This is rare and occurs only on those occasions when you've let your overzealousness for the "right way" rule.

Some may be jealous of you, others will feel honored being around you, but none will argue the importance of your desires and wishes when you've brought them forth from the confines of your mind. They will recognize a power behind your motivations, one of experience and inner spirituality, forces that shed light for those who can recognize them.

7

Numbers Are Related to Physical Characteristics and Health

We've all heard someone else describe a person physically with phrases such as: "Look, isn't she cute! So petite! But I fear a strong wind would come along and blow her away." Or, "His eyes are so deep, I can get lost in them. He's so handsome and tall." And better yet. "His or her slippers could be parked under my bed any day. That person is sexy looking and turns me on!"

All those short descriptions have been heard time and time again. But what do they mean? If one of these statements is made about you, does it make you wonder how you really look to others? How often do you look at yourself in the mirror and scrutinize your physical image?

Below, each explanation pertains to the *general* meaning of the prime digits 1 through 9 and 11, 22, and 33. More specifically, they apply to the Consonant number and the Birthpath number. To find these numbers if you have not done so already, refer to chapters 1 and 5. If, for example, you have a 5 Consonant number and a 3 Birthpath number, *look up both numbers* under this section and blend them together for an even better understanding of your physical attributes and tendencies. You may be surprised at what you discover about yourself.

Number One

In general, you are the type who can burn off calories as quickly as you put them on, though the whole chart of an individual must be taken into consideration. The vigor and assertiveness you possess could also find you burning the candle at both ends through too much activity and a lack of balance. Could it be from too many rendezvous in the moonlight, fervently and energetically courting your companion? It probably is not, and has more to do with pushing and motivating yourself in the career field, the romantic side taking a backseat when success dangles itself like a carrot in front of you.

You don't realize the body mechanism can take only so much. Even Superman knew when to take a break! Your physical and emotional appearance will suffer, which will easily be seen by others, if you challenge yourself to beat the clock without resting in between.

There may be a tendency to scratch your forehead, to fuss with your hair and be quite picky in regard to its style, or you may have a fetish concerning hats. You like to keep your head warm during the cold season, and you can also be prone to tension headaches.

Number Two

Physical motion seems effortless for you, as if you could be walking on air or water. You quite naturally carry yourself with ease and gracefulness.

On the other hand, you may feel clumsy or awkward and unable to move as fluidly as you would like. Don't be too hard on yourself if you feel as if you have two left feet. Just have self-confidence and do some exercising to limber up. That's really all you need—Fred Astaire would love you for it!

The overall body structure may be slim or rounded with a tendency toward weight gain, which could stem from holding water or overeating when nervous or upset. Whether you're thin and trim or pleasingly plump, the general physical appearance is still nice to look at— a defined yet delicate demeanor. Occasionally, some of you may be subject to oily skin.

Number Three

What describes your looks? Your guess is as good as mine! Number 3 never ceases to amaze me in terms of description. One trait is for certain though—youthfulness prevails. This quality, along with sparkling eyes, gives you a charisma all your own. Anageless distinction and childlike innocence surrounds your entire physical presence.

When acting positively, you know how to grow old gracefully and still maintain that youthful zest and charm. On the other hand, when negativity blocks your path, you may cling to a past image of days gone by and spin a web over your appearance.

Personal vanity and constant worry about your age and looks will impede your personal growth. You may even dress in an unbecomingly youthful style and think it looks good. This other side is rare, however. You generally know how to keep that childlike quality, growing older with grace and maturity.

When emotionally out of control, you may be prone to nervousness. Biting your nails, biting your lips, or blowing a minor problem out of proportion may occur when you've decided to let your nerves be the boss. Rashes are not uncommon either. You might also clear your voice nervously, tap your feet, or be subject to attacks of sore throat or laryngitis.

Number Four

Many people seem to be drawn to 4s, both physically and emotionally. You possess a stable and calming presence that is quite attractive to the opposite sex.

Because you have the endurance to handle pressure and not let off steam as situations arise, emotional upsets may be kept hidden. These inward upheavals then manifest themselves through the body instead. Consequently, you may suffer from physical aches and pains of the muscles, stomach, intestinal region, or back area. In addition, I've known number 4 types to develop severe colds because of physical exhaustion or because of inward mental and emotional strain. You may need to express yourself more regularly and not cap emotions unnecessarily!

Your physical characteristics may include a stocky build and broad straight shoulders. The bone structure is considered medium to large. There are, however, some exceptions. I know a few 4s who are medium-boned, have very delicate facial features, and are not stocky, but have a tendency toward a muscular build. Both men and women who are 4 types can develop strong thigh and arm muscles.

Number Five

You are the type who can look quite alluring to the opposite sex. Now, you may not be a Burt Reynolds or a Raquel Welch in physical appearance, but there is something about your image that projects raw sexual charisma; you turn more than a few heads of those who want to take a second look.

Because personal freedom is important as well as the ability to be on the go, you prefer to keep yourself physically fit, remaining a little on the lean side of the scale. You also appreciate a good meal and enjoy it, but occasionally you may find the even distribution tipping slightly to the other end.

As long as the quality is not abused or taken advantage of, you have the ability to bounce back quickly from minor illnesses, i.e., colds, flu, etc. As quickly as you get a virus, that's how fast those minor irritations could dissipate.

The height range is from medium to tall, with some exceptions. Nails and hands are also important and they must be clean. If you're a woman, having your nails long and polished makes you feel more attractive. If you're a man, you are quite finicky about a woman's hands and nails looking feminine.

Number Six

With a 6, height usually ranges from small to medium, therefore, you're probably around 5'2" to 5'6" if a woman and 5'9" to 5'11" if you're a man. Your physical stature is proportioned with curves and hollows in all the right places. You're also light on your feet, a trait shared with the number 5.

There is a tendency toward weight gain as you grow older. It's wise for you to keep meals well-balanced. A sweet tooth is also not uncommon. One of my number 6 clients heads straight for the pastry when hunger strikes, and usually during the late evening hours. He claims he can't help himself, especially if the pastry is topped with chocolate. Enjoying sweets is a quality also shared with the number 3 and 8, and sometimes the number 5. Don't feel too self-conscious, for you are not alone.

Many of you have very delicate skin that needs continual moisture and attention. At times the skin may require a dermatologist's care for a short period. Your general health is good when regular checkups are on the agenda.

Number Seven

You can be fair skinned and very subject to sunburn. There is a fluid yet peaceful look in your eyes, the sort of gaze a person can get lost in.

Many of you have light-colored eyes that are very pronounced. Sometimes the shade of your eyes may change with the color of our clothing. This aspect is shared with a few number 2 types and with some number 9 types. You can be illusionary, possessing transparent qualities that can mirror the image of others if you so desire.

Be cautious when purchasing a pair of shoes, as you need to feel comfortable in footwear. This is shared with some number 3s and 9s I know. The tendency for you to look through rose-colored glasses on occasion may cause you to feel as if you can get away with shoes that are of the latest fad, even though they aren't the best for your feet. If this notion is carried on for too long, at some point in your life it's very possible that you will develop foot problems. A corn here, a callous there, or increasingly poor circulation running from your feet up the knee and beyond is a distinct possibility.

In general, you have a delicate system and should be cautious about overuse of medications, alcohol, etc. At one time or another, you can become quite health conscious to keep the body balanced. Proper foods, vitamins, etc., should become part of your daily diet.

Number Eight

In terms of height, you are probably taller or shorter than the average. Body proportions are either lean and wiry looking or stocky and firm, but you are not necessarily overweight. You do try to balance the scales, yet there still is a tendency toward weight gain later in life. In women, this would affect the stomach and hip area and possibly the lower legs. In men, the addition of weight would definitely show up in the stomach area. Some 8 men would probably make great Santa Clauses!

You are not purposeful walkers; light-footedness may not be one of your better qualities. Consequently, you may wear out your shoes faster than you had expected. You are considered, however, to have excellent control, balance, and rhythm.

You, like the number 7, have a delicate system, regardless of how much stamina and vitality you think you have. When nervous, you could be prone to acid indigestion, heartburn, and upset stomachs. Also, because you have so much energy and would prefer to keep your worries to yourself to maintain your image, the pressure could manifest itself temporarily in a lack of oxygen (hyperventilation) or through the skin (rashes, hives, or short-term swelling).

Number Nine

The 9 is another of the numbers that can recover quickly from minor illnesses. However, your body absorbs what you put into it rather easily. Like the number 7, it would be wise for you to be careful with medications or the absorption of alcoholic beverages, etc. In addition, you should be aware of habits that could get out of your control (eating too much food, smoking too many cigarettes, etc.), especially when under emotional stress.

Like the number 3, you often look younger than your actual chronological age would suggest. You demonstrate a gracious appearance and can be dramatic in gesture and laced with vigor and charm. When involved with worthwhile causes, your enthusiasm can be intoxicating, like the aroma of a well-produced and expensively aged wine.

Number Eleven

Many of you are taller than 5'3", with a few exceptions. Some aspects that make you unique are your energetic manner and highly charged and activated mind. It's difficult for you to keep still and even more of a challenge to stop your train of thought when you've begun talking. When you communicate, it can be quite electric; others may want to stop you from talking so much when you get started but are too fascinated to try. When you strike up a conversation, there's something of an inspirational message hidden between the lines.

You can put on weight quickly or take it off just as fast, depending on whether nervous eating has become a habit.

At times when overextending yourself, you may notice soreness in the calf or ankle. Some of you have a tendency toward weak wrists. (For more information, check number 2 in this chapter.)

Number Twenty-Two

You, like your counterpart 4, are usually medium-boned with a tendency toward physical stamina and endurance. It's interesting to note that many 22s and 4s have natural light brown to dark brown hair. Of course, there are some exceptions.

The opposite sex is drawn to your seemingly stable and somewhat strong personality. Women are attracted to you 22 men because of your ability to protect, safeguard, and demonstrate the macho side of your character. Not all of you want to be macho nor do you think it is necessary, though you play the role if required. Men are attracted to you 22 women because of your consistent, logical, earthy, and sometimes passionate approach to life. You are noted to be the force behind your man at times, whether he wants you to be or not.

Like the number 4, you may experience aches and pains of the muscles when under tension. Other areas of weakness could be the pelvic area or occasionally the reproductive organs. (For more information, check number 4 in this chapter.)

Number Thirty-Three

In physical likeness, you are similar to the number 6. You can appear modest, speaking quietly and choosing your words carefully. Others feel as though they can turn to you and find an understanding friend.

You're dignified in manner, proper in etiquette, and march proudly to the beat of your own drummer. As with the number 6, you must watch the calories later in life and take good care of the delicate skin you possess. Healthwise, you are prone to some type of nervous habit like biting your lips, nails, or timidly stroking your hair. (For more information, check number 6 in this chapter.)

8

Inclusion Table

What is an inclusion table? It's the part or process of the chart that scrutinizes the inner workings of the personality, like looking at the pieces of a puzzle that, when put together, form the total picture.

This chapter provides the ability to separate the generalities from the specifics, the chaff from the wheat—and will highlight a behind-the-door look at the intricacies that mesh together and form your total outward personality.

These intricacies are found through the numbers of the letters of your name. They are the pieces of the puzzle to your own personality. You know these traits and are familiar with how to blend them together in producing your outward self. The inclusion table depicts those qualities that enhance your uniqueness, helping to describe what makes you different from everybody else.

The prime digits are 1 through 9. In each given name at birth, find out how many 1s for example (which represent leadership), 2s (which represent cooperation), 3s (which represent the qualities of imagination), etc., you have in the name. *If there is a number missing, it means that there is a lesson to be learned regarding those qualities represented by that missing numeral.*

97

In some respects, the missing numbers indicate a karmic lesson. If we can accept the possibility of reincarnation, then it suggests that in previous incarnations you either overdid yourself in those areas or paid no attention to them at all. Now you will be asked to try again and hopefully this time get it right.

For those of you who are skeptical regarding reincarnation, I suggest this alternate explanation: the stages of learning from birth to the present, hidden within your personality, are the necessary tools represented by this missing number. Life itself will test your judgment and ability to develop these characteristics from the weak to the strong. Actual situations and experiences will push you into areas where the conditions of the missing number must be met, but as always, you have the choice to learn them when presented or at another time.

Mind you, learning is never easy, especially if you don't like what you are being taught. Training ourselves to respond to the qualities listed in the inclusion table will make learning that much easier.

We as humans are goal-seeking beings who desire perfection, but the most ideal side of ourself cannot be learned overnight. It may take what seems to be lifetimes to reach that state of Divine Harmony and universal perfection we seek.

There are two schools of life: the school of hard knocks and the school of observation. The inclusion table tells you what some of the subjects will be. You can make it as easy or as hard on yourself as you like. Those conditions, nonetheless, will still come up.

We will break down a name and the personality traits to gain an even better insight into you as an individual. Let's take an example to illustrate how it works.

```
A L I C E   H E N D E R S O N
1 3 9 3 5   8 5 5 4 5 9 1 6 5
```

INCLUSION TABLE

(1)	(2)	(3)
2	0	2
(4)	(5)	(6)
1	5	1
(7)	(8)	(9)
0	1	2

As you can see, the inclusion table incorporates all the nine numbers (marked in parentheses) and under each is the amount that Alice has in her given name at birth. Example, Alice has two number 1s, no number 2s, etc. Remember to use the name as it appears on the birth certificate; first, middle (if you have one), and last. This will be the only way you're sure to be accurate in your analyzation. I will again give you the scale of letters to numbers so that you can apply the proper assignations to your birth name.

```
1 2 3 4 5 6 7 8 9
A B C D E F G H I
J K L M N O P Q R
S T U V W X Y Z
```

I call this process the "almighty" inclusion table, for without its use your knowledge will be more general than specific.

In short, the inclusion table aids in focusing on what you have to your credit and what you'll need to work on to keep the balance sheet in check. If, for example, *your Birthpath number matches one of those numerals within the letters*, it indicates that you're learning through the experiences of life an even better way to use those qualities presented through the name.

For instance, let's say that in the example of Alice Henderson, she has the birthdate of March 7, 1960.

$$\begin{array}{r} 1960 \\ 7 \\ + \ 3 \\ \hline 1970 \end{array} \ / \ 1+9+7+0 \ = \ 17 \ / \ 1+7 \ = \ 8 \ \text{Birthpath}$$

Alice has an 8 Birthpath number, but she also has an 8 in her name (see inclusion table). Therefore, Alice is rediscovering how to utilize the qualities of the executive and the organizer, and to pursue the goals indicated by the Birthpath number in another way— through a higher level of operation. It also indicates that she will strain a little harder for the security and the control she desires because she has an 8 in both the Birthpath position and in the letters of the birthname. It intensifies those qualities, yet aids in tapping her inner nature more quickly.

Keep the Birthpath in mind when scrutinizing the inclusion table. If one of the numbers in that table matches your Birthpath numeral, then the diamond you have is polished. Let's see how brilliant it becomes through the new learning experiences of the Birthpath.

Below is an explanation of each of the numbers represented in the inclusion table.

Number One

WITH—There is a strong drive for leadership and independence with 1s present. Once a decision is made, you'll surge ahead. You don't like to be told what to do and prefer to operate within your own framework of originality. You consider yourself balanced in your approach to self-reliance and dependence. You strive to put forth your ideas with exuberance and a pioneering spirit, yet at the same time you do understand that being too bossy or dominant will get you nowhere in a hurry. The balance of push and pull is constantly weighed and measured. More than two or three 1s in a name will strike notes of a strong ego; the self is accented more than you would like to admit. Too many 1s within the name will caution you not to overdo your role as leader. You could find yourself possessing a kingdom without subjects if you play king or queen of the mountain too enthusiastically.

WITHOUT—This is a mini-lesson regarding your fight for individuality. One minute you can be overly zealous, and the next, hide the drive necessary to stand on your own two feet and be counted. Life will teach you how to effect the symmetry of doing things your own way and when to back off and take a break. You may be called upon to lead projects, initiate action, or begin a brand-new life, but you will be tested on what means you use to accomplish your goals. Will you run roughshod over others, or will you take the reins of control through persistent and objective methods? You will be tested on when to brilliantly shine in the light of attention that says, "Hey, look at me," and when to let it dimly flicker.

Number Two

WITH—You are a sensitive creature who can cover your sensitivity with other facets of your personality. Within your framework lies a very gentle spirit, seeking harmony in cooperative pursuits. You understand that persuasion through diplomacy will bring the desired result much faster than using obstinancy, especially when there are more than two 2s in the name. There is great importance placed on the little things. Your ideals and constant subtle quest for harmony may find you wearing your heart on your sleeve more often than not. That's fine as long as you can keep from bandying it about—a tough task, particularly if there are many 2s in the name. At times, you may have trouble making decisions. Why? Because you can be so objective in seeing both sides of an issue, making a final judgment is difficult. You truly desire peace and kinship among co-workers, friends, and loved ones.

WITHOUT—Here lies a small lesson on objectivity and emotional balance, and on learning to develop your sensitivities so as not to go to extremes. On the one hand, you can walk a mile in someone else's shoes, and on the other, you might not even want to test the fit. Life will show you how to even out the scale of emotional justice. Deep within the personality is a longing for closeness and a desire to belong to someone special. Yet, with the missing 2 you are more apt to project a delicate but defensive wall toward objects of your affection than to open up and let the sea of feeling float you upon its current. It's at those times others may not recognize how deeply caring and sensitive you really are. If you are a man with no 2s in the name, then you may not understand women and all their wiles and ways. If you are a woman with no 2s, it may be easier to associate with men and enjoy their conversations. Overall, you will be taught through life's experiences the value of your own self-confidence. Like plucking a rose from a thicket of thorns, the pinpricks of life will only be temporary when you recognize that securing the rose was worth it after all.

Number Three

WITH—You have a wonderful gift of gab, coupled with a vivid imagination that weaves its web through the spinning of your tales of experience. Having a flair for the dramatic, you'll anoint your goals, friendships, and loves with optimistic and fanciful gestures. You want to be noticed and to involve yourself in the lime-light in some way, sharing the joys bubbling inside you. The warning here, however, is not to take on too much, especially if you have more than two 3s in your name. If this happens, you'll start many projects but finish few of them. Like a butterfly who flits from bush to flower, you'll extend your social graces and sense of humor to those who cross your path in the wind. You'll dab your practicality with lightheartedness and goodwill. You recognize the value of laughing at yourself and the foibles of life, expressing the knowledge that in every gray cloud there is a silver lining. If 3s are pronounced within the name, the artistic abilities you possess can shine like a beacon. Writing, music, and the arts in some way will beckon you at some point to their path, even if only for a short while.

WITHOUT—Flowery metaphors and "coffee klatch" crowds don't seem to be your style. You are more serious of mind, not realizing that deep within your personality creativity lies in abundance. Others will say, "You can do it." You'll say, "No, I can't. I'm not that creatively inclined." So, you may not fancy yourself as an entrepreneur of entertainment or a writer of romances, etc., feeling more comfortable with the how-to kind of things. You will appreciate those who have real talent, because you may think you do not. This is wrong! Life will teach you to bring out what's really inside—creative expression. Inwardly there is a lack of self-worth, not just a lack of self-confidence; so you'll need to be pushed to a degree. Through trial and error, you'll grow more comfortable with your talents and optimistic expectations. On occasion you may display a pessimistic attitude, wondering if the sun will ever shine. It will if you let it in. As you travel down the road, experiences will pop out from behind hill and dale, asking you to bring out your sense of humor and joy in situations with children, brothers, sisters, and loved ones. In career or work you may be called upon, for example, to write a story, think of an advertising campaign, plan a children's party, etc., all of it done to extricate your creative abilities.

Number Four

WITH—Your sense of duty and responsibility can be either your friend or your foe. If you have more than one 4 in the name, then the workaholic syndrome becomes more pronounced. Although you possess outstanding integrity, loyalty, and perseverance, you may not know when to quit. You are an excellent manager of others' affairs, but you may not enjoy the prospect of delegating something you're involved in to someone else. Why? Because you feel that if you hand it over, the project or plan may not be completed in the right fashion. So, you'll hesitate or have a tendency to supervise anything you've turned over to someone else. This means that you can be tenacious with tasks, your money, and even your loved ones. You have an enduring quality; you *can* go the distance. You're a hard worker, and that's why you can become exhausted or anxious! And you do worry—about everything. Practicing a one-step-at-a-time attitude benefits your progress. With many 4s, family, friends, and especially in-laws add either more pleasure or more pain to existing conditions.

WITHOUT—You work equally hard, but in short spurts. You'll tackle a project you like for eighteen hours instead of eight, then put it down. Because of the enormous energy it took, you may not get back to that task again; so you go to extremes. Either you work too hard or not enough. You will learn a lesson in discipline. Make a daily to-do list; start organizing yourself on a regular basis. This includes your finances as well as your dreams and your daily schedule at home, for life at some point will test your efficiency. You want security and a firm foundation, yet there is a part of your personality that fears any type of restriction or limitation. You can worry either too much or not at all. You may dislike physical labor (unless you have help by a 4 in another position) or working with your hands. Through your experiences you will gain an understanding of the meaning of the number 4 and the necessity of boundaries and what routine means to you. By gaining the proper knowledge of structure through a consistent and steadfast approach, you're sure to come out a winner.

Number Five

WITH—Within your personality lies a gypsy at heart. Not inclined toward the conventional, the traits you bring out are freedom seeking, progressive, and different. You like to go places, search out answers to your curious questions, and maintain a flexibility in relationships and work. Although you may be able to handle a nine-to-five routine with ease, you exude the desire for variety on the job. At home, you won't like to sit still. You've got this feeling of motion and activity as one of your idiosyncracies. With more than three 5s in the name, you may change your mind more often than you wish. Too many 5s in the name indicates an abundance of nervous energy and the desire for self-promotion and working in the public eye. Many 5s within the name warns you not to be a "rolling stone that gathers no moss," but rather to emphasize the ability to be a free thinker, unlocking the chains of restriction and bondage and understanding the necessity of securing a lasting foundation.

WITHOUT—Sometimes you may seem to be like a stuffed shirt, talking about the tried and true and taking totally conservative approaches. On other occasions you'll simply cast your fate to the wind, drinking in experiences from the uncorked bottle of sensualized pleasure and unusual experiences. Herein lies a lesson of balance between your disciplined self and your free-loving attitudes. Life, your teacher, has made you change, grow, and be flexible through moves, emergencies, and the invasion of friends into your realm of living. All the while, it has maneuvered the strings to keep you in a continuous check and balance. By presenting you with new places to go, different people to see, and a variety of things to do, you've had to deal with progress and meet it face to face. Sitting still is not allowed, but neither is purposeless activity. You are here to learn to proper use of personal freedom.

Number Six

WITH—Your personality hints at protectiveness and a guiding parental attitude. You have the ability to adjust your affairs to suit the needs of others. Beauty, luxury, and the desire for harmonious and emotionally strong family ties are considered important, particularly with more than two 6s within the name. Many 6s will caution you not to be overly protective or to force your ideals upon others. There is a tendency toward possessiveness when 6s are pronounced. Service to the family, community, or the country may call you to be responsible. Neighbors and pets can surround you with love and friendliness. Some of your idiosyncracies include a pickiness for perfection, especially in the kitchen, and in the way you take care of the house. You can be a disciplinarian, yet those you love know all the angles to get around your rules. You're a softy at heart. You usually enjoy eating excellently prepared meals and may be considered a gourmet in your own right. Making a house a home with all its comforts is a trait worth having, and you certainly do—without question.

WITHOUT—Life will call upon you to serve your masters, which are responsibility, obligation, and devotion. The missing 6 is a call to develop balance between your emotional security of self and your service to others. Because you have no 6s, your home may have that comfortable lived-in look. You're not as picky about putting things away as soon as they have been used or about washing the dishes immediately after eating. Those things you'll take in stride. Domestic strife will also be taken more lightly because you know full well that "this too shall pass." Experience as a teacher will ask you to share and bring forth your love through a sense of duty. Having a good marriage through give and take, as well as administering advice and solving dilemmas for yourself and others, will be expected until you learn the lesson of responsibility through lending a hand.

Number Seven

WITH—To have a 7 within the name is a gift. Many people (based on the English language) have none. It represents both the intellectual and intuitive processes. You believe in covering your backside while you search for the hidden messages veiled within the answers. For you, if plan A does not work, you've got a backup alternative. Too many 7s caution you not to try to rationalize your way out of trouble. You're great at that! Anything you want seems to be right as long as you can apply the rationale to fit it. A 7 within the name indicates a trait of mental perfection; it is the searcher of higher truth and knowledge. You have the ability to read through the actions of others, coupled with the balance of blending reason with intuition. You have your own philosophies about religion and what faith is. Mystical yet technical, you'll analyze higher law. At times this may confuse you. You can believe purely by faith but at the same time challenge it because you want it to be proven. Too many 7s caution you not to fight what you do not understand, nor to ignore your fine gift of perception by overanalyzing what you perceive in feeling. Too many 7s should recognize the value of saying, "I feel" instead of "I think."

WITHOUT—You can apply your feelings of intuition to everyday life and come out on top each time. The only difficulty here is you don't always trust what you perceive. So, you'll rely on others to reassure you of what you already know. Overall, you are open-minded and perceptive about higher law and spiritual awakening. The belief in God can be very strong, but so can thinking you will be punished severely if you stray from the path of righteousness. The missing 7 means balance is needed between logic and intuition, and to delve further into things, taking the time to analyze thoroughly before you jump the gun. With this number missing, there are times you may put on rose-colored glasses, seeing illusion where you think reality exists. By using both your spiritual and mental qualities in harmony, any fears about yourself, your beliefs, or your goals will dissipate like water that turns to vapor, relinquishing itself into the air. You may also have a fear of being lonely. Do not be afraid of being separate, for there is a difference between being alone and being lonely. Life will test your ability to distinguish between the two. It will teach you to feel secure within yourself. Experiences will show you the value of being content to spend time alone. In these periods of downtime, you will find inner peace and a reenergizing of your own life force. You will be able to walk, refreshed, back into the hustle and bustle of everyday living.

Number Eight

WITH—The traits of organization, control, and authority are present. You may at times feel like the executive in charge. You know how to make a deal by getting the most for your money and have the ability to discern between a scam and the real thing. You may on occasion have to repeat your efforts to secure your position, but you will also recognize the need to be sure of your tracks by going over them again. You have the ability to balance out your spiritual beliefs with your material inclinations, producing ethics by keeping one foot in higher law and the other foot in the physical/monetary realm of existence. Too many 8s caution you not to strain after glory, power, or money for fear of its loss. All those things will be harder and harder to obtain until you realize that the more you let go, through accomplishment for yourself and others, the more you will get back in return. It warns you not to venture after money purely for money's sake. When 8s are pronounced, tremendous inner drive is indicated. It can be a controlled power that reaches many. Having 8s in the name may find you fearing death or feeling reluctant to discuss a life after. This is because you challenge yourself with the unseen world—is it there or isn't it? Once you've gained understanding in these areas, you'll grow more comfortable with the knowledge of the divine plan.

WITHOUT—For one thing, life will teach you how to handle your own money, but not always someone else's. You may find yourself having the cash and then losing it once again until you master this ability. You have your own system when it comes to your checkbook. Granted, the total is always accurate, but how you arrived at it may not be understood by anyone else but you. Little things such as how your charge account works, how to budget your money consistently and how much or little you spend on an item all come under this lesson's scrutiny. One minute you worry about lack of cash, and the next you have an inner faith that it will be provided when needed (some people with 8s should take a lesson from you in this last respect). In the past, you may have ignored commercial or business means or have abused their application. Life will now teach you to value your own personal judgments at the same time that it throws you into a position of authority, even if only temporarily. Why? To school you in making proper decisions and managing things by yourself. You will be taught the value of getting what you deserve—no more, no less—and to realize the importance of using the gifts of wealth, recognition, and achievement for the good of all concerned.

Number Nine

WITH—Hidden within your personality lies a generosity of spirit. You can mix and mingle with people of different walks of life due to your impersonal objective attitudes. At times you will be called upon to complete what others have started. Many 9s in the name suggest you are highly impressionable and extremely idealistic, full of sensitivity, emotion, and feeling. With many 9s you may be prone to wanting the limelight, being extremely dramatic and gifted with creativity, yet you may be prone to scattering energy and to a lack of direction. That's when you need to swing back to the realities of a situation to put you back on track. An abundance of 9s warns you not to be fickle, moody, or to dream your life away. It also indicates worldly experience through travel, situations, or study, coupled with a keen perception that looks deep within another's nature. You can feel what others feel. A truly empathic and humanitarian quality will be accented.

WITHOUT—This missing number indicates a lesson on impersonal love, which calls you to put aside selfishness and purely personal gain to extend your love to many through selflessness. Now this is not to say that a missing 9 means you have to be a saint. It suggests that giving without thought of return is expected in order for you to gain an appreciation of the value of sharing, which you may not have done in the past. In addition, you will be asked to regulate the emotional side of your nature.

Your feelings should not be repressed, yet your control will be tested in the expression of these emotions. Like a faucet with a valve, learn to manipulate the outpouring of affection, so that you can steady the stream. Until this is learned, you will go to extremes in your emotional expectations, experiencing highs and lows. Purely subjective and personal attitudes will not be allowed, for you will notice that anything that enhances those attributes will be taken from you until you come to the recognition of impersonal love and giving. The missing 9 asks you to broaden your outlook by learning the importance of different walks of life, getting a good education, and continuing to seek and express a worldly attitude. You own everything and nothing at the same time; this is the lesson to be learned.

9

Pinnacles

Two other areas we'll take a look at are found from the birth date and are called the Pinnacles and the Challenges. This chapter will be devoted to the explanation of the Pinnacles, how to find them and what they mean.

The Pinnacles of Life indicate those experiences that will be confronting you during their transit. In fact, by knowing how to set this up, you will be able to see the patterns and trends of life as they take shape and weave their way through the Pinnacles. During their transit you will also take on some of the qualities of that number, which will aid you in dealing with new situations. This process is one part of a chart to be looked at for forecasting. However, it covers approximately a nine-year span, with the exception of the first and last Pinnacle, so you will need to be aware that the interpretations are more general than specific.

There are four Pinnacles of Life. To find them, from your birthdate

1. Add the month and day of birth only. Reduce to one number. This is the first Pinnacle of Life.
2. Add the day and year together only and reduce to one number. This is the second Pinnacle of Life.
3. Add the first and second Pinnacles together, once

again reducing to one number. You now have the third Pinnacle.

4. Add the month of birth and the year of birth only and reduce to one number to acquire the fourth Pinnacle of Life.

As understood in previous chapters, reduce all compounds to one digit in the pinnacles with the exception of the master numbers 11, 22 and 33.

To find the timing of the Pinnacles, that is, how long each Pinnacle is in operation, employ the following:

1. Begin with what is considered the given number 36 (4 x 9), and subtract from your Birthpath number (total of your birthdate) from it. *If your Birthpath is an 11, 22 or 33, then reduce* it to the prime digit *before* subtracting it from 36. (The given number 36 is also the chronological age generally determined as the midway point at which individuals may set their base or foundation for life.) The number that is left is the age when the first Pinnacle ends. It is always the Birthpath number that is subtracted from the given (age) 36.

   Now add one year. (Adding one year takes into consideration the time from actual birth to age 1.) The number that is left is the age when the first Pinnacle ends.

2. From the end of that first Pinnacle add nine years, which covers the duration of the second Pinnacle.

3. From the end of the second Pinnacle add another nine years. This is the time span for the third Pinnacle.

4. The fourth and final Pinnacle of Life is from the end of the third Pinnacle through the remainder of your life.

Let's take an example. This illustration is that of the late John Lennon. His birthdate is as follows:

PINNACLES

$$\frac{6}{6} \quad \frac{\text{49 to end of life}}{\text{40 to 49}}$$

0 to 31 $\quad \underline{1} \quad \overline{5} \quad \underline{\text{31 to 40}}$

October 9, 1940

10/1 $\quad$ 9 $\quad$ 14/5 = 6 Birthpath

By his birthdate, we see that John Lennon's first Pinnacle was at 1, which ran the lengthy span from birth to age 31. It was during this time that he became one of The Beatles and was considered the leader of that group. It was known that through this stage John was somewhat of a rebel, very independent and an original thinker. He wasn't afraid to take chances or to express his thoughts and ideas. This typically describes some of the experiences of the number 1 in this first position. Although he went through a stormy and radical time during his teens (his father left the family when John was young), he pushed himself to the top and strove to be recognized and valued. The mark he made in life was accomplished through his music. A 1 Pinnacle brings with it the chance to forge ahead through self-determination and pioneering efforts.

Through the Pinnacles you can time your best chances and opportunities for success by following the general guidelines put forth through their interpretations. For example, if your first Pinnacle is a 9 and you decide you want to get married, it would be best to remember that your marriage would be one of service and dealing with the public in some way. In other words, it might not be a white-house-and-picket-fence type of relationship, where dinner would be cooking at the same time each day or the regular arrival of your mate could be expected. No, 9 rules people and impersonal love, throwing you into situations that call for the kind of service in which schedules would vary for both of you.

If your second Pinnacle, however, happens to be a 6 and you want a marriage that includes family and all the trimmings (pets, neighbors, community service, etc.), then marrying during that time would be much better. Why? Number 6 rules home and family and would be more conducive to a regulated routine and home-type endeavors.

As the Pinnacles change, so will you to a degree. Situations, experiences, obligations, and feelings will take on the color of those traits represented by the number transiting through in the Pinnacles. This will flavor or costume your nature to an extent. As another example: you want to start your own business, but are not sure when. Your first Pinnacle of Life is a 7. Your second Pinnacle of Life is an 8. What do you think you should do based on what you've already read? You guessed it. Generally speaking, wait until that second Pinnacle comes into operation before you cast the dice and begin your commercial enterprise, for that's exactly what an 8 rules (along with values and ethics). It would be appropriate, and you would stand a better chance of succeeding during this second Pinnacle transit than you would during the first.

Now, this is not to say that any year during that 8 Pinnacle would be all right. There are better years than others during its transit; so the rest of the chart needs to be scrutinized (i.e., personal year, essences, etc., which are not covered in this book) and more specific timing given. By generally checking this transit, it would prove to be a better overall time in which to proceed along business lines.

It's important to note that you should take these Pinnacle numbers into consideration with the rest of the numbers you've learned about thus far to create a more accurate picture.

For example, if one of your Pinnacles is an 8, yet that number is missing in the letters of the name as well as elsewhere, then during that Pinnacle transit you will

be offered many opportunities in the arena of business
plus the potential of making more money and learning
more about value choices. You will also receive lessons
about those very activities to balance out what you're
missing. That Pinnacle will be an intense one, and those
experiences will most assuredly transpire in order to
perfect those qualities in you—one way or another!

Here's another example: say your Birthpath number matched one of those Pinnacles. You will find ease
and opportunity with those situations and feelings,
because you will be naturally drawn into your purpose in life and will have a chance to draw out your
innermost talents. It would be your power time.
When the Birthpath matches any forecasting number
through transit position (like the Pinnacles), you can
come out smelling like a rose *if* you follow what it
dictates. There would be protection and a natural
push along these lines.

Remember to keep in mind that the Pinnacles
should be used in conjunction with other numbers
within your name and birth date. For example, if your
Pinnacle matches the Vowel number in the name, it
indicates you will have potential and opportunities to
realize some of your desires. If the Pinnacle matches
the total of your name, then your outward personality
will be accented during its transit and so will career
endeavors suited to those patterns on a more consistent basis. If the Pinnacle matches your Consonant
number, then the facade you put forth will be accented and so might some of your secret dreams and
wishes.

Below is an explanation of each of the numbers as
they apply to the Pinnacles of Life. There will be general discussions given on each, as the period covered
entails a number of years. It would benefit you to apply
the depictions, for you will notice their influence within
your own life.

Number One Pinnacle

This is a time when you are asked to forge ahead. In many instances, a 1 Pinnacle will find you having to start over; a complete change of life-style begins to overtake your existing conditions. You can be like a thoroughbred waiting at the starting line for the gates to fling open and free the horses to run the race. Situations come in rapidly that allow you to move to the top of the ladder. However, don't procrastinate. It will require courage and keen mental deciphering for you to separate the scam from the real thing. A 1 Pinnacle will give you the ability to go after what you want. Males may be accented at this time and prove to be beneficial through support or service. But things won't be handed to you on a silver platter during this cycle; you'll need to search them out. Planning is the key, not impulsiveness. You will be like Johnny Appleseed, planting the ideas, scanning the land, penetrating the soil of action with the seeds of your conceptions. Remember, a seed takes root and later a flower blooms.

A 1 Pinnacle is quite literally a period of planting new things and possibly a new life-style through independent action and originality of thought. Bossiness or dominance will only bring heartache and separations, and may cause you to topple from your platform. Self-reliance and constructive goals that are pioneered with fortitude will pay off in dollars later on. You have the reins that control the horse in the race. What position do you want to be in at the finish line: win, place, or show? It's up to you.

Number Two (Eleven) Pinnacle

Yours is "not to reason why," yours is "but to . . ." wait and be patient! Now that the seeds have been planted, let them germinate and grow rich within the soil. Whether you're electrically overloaded with sudden happenings (if the Pinnacle is an 11) or quietly pursuing your aims (if the Pinnacle is a 2), don't butt your head against the wall or try to defy what will only take time. Things already started may have their chance at successful completion, but some of the flowers of your efforts still need a little more watering.

In this Pinnacle, you'll find yourself dealing with associations and organizations, playing an effective role through peaceful persuasion, inspirational zeal, and team spirit. Women in particular are highly accented, many of whom could prove to be beneficial by offering opportunity.

There will be times of sensitivity. You're more idealistic now. Romance, the flicker of candlelight, and the moon in all its shining glory can whisk you away in moments of heartfelt love and endearing thoughts and gestures.

Often you won't feel like eating a heavy meal and may prefer light appetizers or dining on smaller portions. However, weight gain is possible through either nervous eating or water retention. You will be paying close attention to detail during this time and the little things will be important to you and others as well. Emotional balance and general objectivity both take a turn in this Pinnacle. Don't let yourself be used as a doormat, but do understand the meaning of "taking a backseat" once in a while.

An 11 Pinnacle can accentuate the intuition in the same way a 2 can, and spiritual, religious, or philosophical learnings can be experienced. This Pinnacle could just as easily throw you into the limelight, where you're the center of attention. You'll sometimes wonder how you attained acclaim; it seemed to happen so quickly!

Whether you are in a 2 or an 11 Pinnacle, use yourself like a magnet to attract the metal of success. Opportunity will come easier by not pushing too demandingly, yet it will not tolerate vacillation either.

If it's meant to be, you won't have to look far; success will present itself to you with open arms.

Number Three Pinnacle

This proves to be a very active and fertile time when the flower of life blooms. Love and marriage with all the fanfare, bridal showers, ceremonies, and babies are signs of the times.

If what you've been sincerely working on seemed to be a little uncertain before now, anticipate no longer. The petals of success will open now, and your rose will emit its fragrance. The aromas of success could manifest in increased earnings, unexpected gifts, or words of praise and recognition. A 3 Pinnacle will, if deserved, put you in the limelight.

During this time, you may decide to become involved in creative pursuits. You could paint your home or apartment, improve your appearance, party with your friends, entertain, or be entertained by attending shows, plays, or musical concerts. In addition, a 3 could accent your psychic abilities or clairvoyant tendencies. It's a colorful period full of friends, brothers, sisters, and dramatic, optimistic attitudes.

Like a child in an amusement park, you may never tire of wanting to have a good time, but be careful not to burn the candle at both ends or to scatter your precious energy. During this Pinnacle you may be tempted to leave projects unfinished because of interruptions. A 3 will demand that you complete what you started in thought, word, or deed.

Number Four (Twenty-Two) Pinnacle

March, march, march to discipline, dedication, and the enjoyment of a job well done. Now begins the process of digging up the soil, turning it over, and reworking an area for planting of new seeds. The work may

119

be hard but is well worth the effort. This is a period of transformation, either large or small.

Paperwork, projects, home, foundations, even in-laws and relatives may be spotlighted. The 4 Pinnacle of Life asks you to be organized and yet to take things as they come—one step at a time. If pushing too hard, your health could be affected through muscle aches and pains or physical exhaustion. Diligently applying yourself is one thing, but overdoing it is another. If you become too hung up on perfection for the sake of something being right, or worry about every little detail, then you'll end up working harder and not smarter. As long as you understand that the 4 asks you to regulate and maintain order and a routine in your goals and actions, you'll find yourself meeting the demands of this period comfortably, without experiencing the anxieties produced by pressure and responsibility.

In a 4 or 22 Pinnacle, standing up for the principle of something will be spotlighted on occasion. You'll feel a little more serious-minded and intent on standing up for what you believe. It requires you also to bend but not break; so compromise may be the order of the day. You must realize when to let go of old habits and patterns of security that are outdated and no longer useful and when to retain those that are.

This Pinnacle of Life is a concrete-laying time. You are pouring in the liquid cement of foundation on which to build a better road to success. You will develop the sweat of hard work and routine either mentally, physically, or emotionally, but you ultimately will have made your dreams come true. When your structures are completed, no one will be able to crack the framework you've molded.

Number Five Pinnacle

Freedom, activity, and change can be promised in this Pinnacle. Like a person who goes through a meadow of flowers plucking the petals of his or her choice, you will have the opportunity to seek out and experience different facets of living. It can be a very exciting and adventurous time.

Number 5 rules the mind as well as the body. During this period, you will discover parts of yourself that crave answers to your curiosities. You want to improve your health, engage in extra physical exercise, or experience the excitement of living.

People will walk in and out of your life sharing a petal or two of experience and adding to your collection of knowledge. Having more than one iron in the fire is not uncommon during this time, but be aware that "too many cooks spoil the broth." If you don't heed the warning, you may stroll out of this period knowing a little bit about a lot of things but a whole lot about nothing. This Pinnacle can prove to be as exhausting or invigorating as you will allow it to be.

The senses are more activated. Your senses of taste and touch, for example, draw you into embracing the new and different. Sexual activity could increase, and romance livens up stagnant conditions, but again there is a warning: be discriminating, otherwise you could encounter unusual or very strange experiences. The way to use your personal freedom and flexibility will be put to the test. Now is the time to bend like the willow, except the unexpected, go with the flow of living, and be able to stay in the mainstream, limber and elastic, adept at dodging the rocks and boulders.

The key word is progress, which includes changes of job, life-style, and/or location. All of this is designed to break open the cocoon and free the butterfly in all its radiant colors.

Number Six (Thirty-Three) Pinnacle

A vase of flowers sits on the table. It has been taken care of with love and nurturing care because the blossoms are a beauty to behold. The flowers are protected,

Karen J. David

watered, and plucked of any impediments and dried leaves by someone who is responsible for them.

Like the person who takes good care of things of beauty, you pass through this period a helpmate, a counselor, and a humanitarian to family, friends, and the public.

Number 6 accents marriage, divorce, children, dwellings, and making a house a home. Neighbors and pets may also enter the picture, leaving an imprint on your memory during this time.

In a 6 Pinnacle, you may find the mate you will marry. On the other, hand you could remain single. Does that sound ironic? It is a little, but in searching for the ideal mate, your pedestal of perfection and expectations may be too high. What happens? You end up alone. Preserving your principles of beauty and your ideals are crucial, but being too picky and finding fault with those you love may find you living alone, embittered, and overladen with unwanted burdens. Accepting people as they are, not as you would like them to be, is the principle that is required.

A 33 Pinnacle still demands community or family service from you, but the energy of this combination is dynamic and restless. You want to sit still yet can't seem to do so. It draws you into larger arenas of service, usually to the public, and will ask you to teach others through setting examples. It won't be just lip service or preaching about your beliefs; you'll be required to be a living example of them.

Whether a 6 or 33 Pinnacle, there is a homey feeling around you. The desire to entertain more in the home, conduct your field of business from the house, or improve your home in whatever fashion necessary will permeate the air. Lending a helping hand could pay off in later rewards. Giving service to the military, for example, or teaching, writing, schooling, or caring for someone who is not feeling well, all can be part of this experience.

This Pinnacle is a fine time for developing harmo-

122

nious experiences and relationships, ones which meet
the ideals set, promising reward in return for the responsibility and caring of others. The key is to accept
what is already there, not make it into something it is
not. You will then have a wonderful period of love,
happiness, glowing contentment, and fulfilling service.
It is a time that can render scenes of a soft rug, warm
fireplace, and a snuggling hug of love amid a peaceful
atmosphere. All you need to do is accept the task and
serve with a smile!

Number Seven Pinnacle

Hear the whisper of the breeze, the sound of the
waves as they roll in toward shore, and the rustle of the
leaves in the wind. Keep your rudder steady as you sail
quietly centered, deep in thought, and marveling at the
wonder of nature and all her majesty. This is what a 7
Pinnacle can be like. It can also present you with the
snap, crackle, and pop of a busy period, jaunting this
way and that as you persevere, struggling to meet dead-
lines, responsibilities, and success. It electrically charges
the circuits of situations with sudden decisions and
analytical problem solving.

In either case, you will soul search through introspection. It represents the student thinker both inwardly and outwardly. During this time, you will be
offered the opportunity to regroup, refine, and perfect
who you are, but it is not an interval to be impulsive
or put on rose-colored glasses. Number 7 represents the
reality and the illusion, and you must discern the difference. This period can deal with others in relation to
yourself, legalities, politics, and contracts, and suggests
that you avoid speculative risks.

During this transit, you may feel quieter than usual
and may not seem to have all the answers to the questions of others, although you will certainly have opinions. You see, you've entered a period of serious mental
contemplation and house cleaning, separating in your

mind what is necessary and what is not. Others may perceive this as being secretive, opinionated, or mysterious. Hence, misunderstandings can also arise. Hidden problems or opportunities, especially those which have stagnated or have been left aside, will be rekindled. This could rule health, emotions, relationships, or career.

It's a time to learn how to relax and enjoy the peacefulness of being alone. This transmitting period urges you to get out into the country or anywhere close to the land or the sea. By doing so you will be refreshed, once away from the madding crowd. Intuition through nature and all her gems will hold answers and will heal you.

You won't want to be amid noise and confusion regularly, nor will you find yourself constantly in the mainstream of the jet-setting crowd. On occasion, you'll have just as much fun enjoying the comforts of solitude. You may research subjects on philosophy, metaphysics, or technical topics, improving the mind through analyzation and digging to the root of a question or problem. You are more apt to ask why instead of what. Regulate your tempo to be calm, cool, and collected as you pass through this Pinnacle.

Number Eight Pinnacle

The seeds have been planted, the crop has matured and is now ripe and ready for harvesting. This is what your 8 Pinnacle will provide—the reaping of what you have sown through endurance and effort. It repays in direct proportion to what has been expended in time, money, value, and commitment. If you've done your best for yourself and for all those concerned and are continuing to do so, this Pinnacle will prove to be most rewarding.

The 8 rules a meshing of the material and spiritual aspects, a push for the top through the proper value choices. Questions on spirituality, religion, or life and death could spark interest in pursuing an understanding of higher law. Educational, commercial, and general business opportunities make themselves known. An 8 demands the best judgment possible and will ask repeated efforts from you to reach your ultimate aims.

During this transit, you can gain respect and help from people in influential positions. Eyes will be on you and your performance. Money and its concerns will crop up in some manner. It can rule your monetary possessions or other people's money in relation to you and may be in the form of insurance, inheritances, pay increases, and outside investments. It's a busy, active period, one in which you will feel the pressure of responsibility and planning through delegation. Because of all the hustle and bustle of important tasks, don't be surprised if you find yourself talking in tangents. Your ideas move faster than your completed sentences. You could be asked to head projects or manage and supervise a business. You may be called upon to give your opinions on finances or the decisions of others.

You can be a good judge of character at this time, but it also cautions you not to be both judge and jury. The 8 rules power and how to control it. You have the capacity to influence greatly now, as well as the opportunity to be thrown into important responsibility and the limelight from an executive standpoint. You could become egotistical, too proud, or headstrong if you have not learned how to weigh and measure the responsibility of this command. If not balanced, the tower will crumble, leaving things in little pieces that you will be required to pick up and put back together. Health is also a consideration. Straining for success or excessive worry in money matters will take a toll on your emotional and physical makeup. Again, balance is the key, and by maintaining this symmetry, you'll enter and leave this period with security, success, and position.

Number Nine Pinnacle

The fall is changing to winter. You cover the ground with straw to protect the rich soil for next season's planting and care for those shrubs you've tended for some time now. Pruning the area of waste, dead leaves, branches, and stones, you're preparing a space that will be ready to germinate the seeds of future gardens.

Don't be alarmed at the regular use of statements such as "I don't know" or "We'll wait and see." When transiting this Pinnacle, you will use those sentences more than once. You see, a 9 Pinnacle can be one of the best or one of the worst times to go through. It all depends on how well you understand the qualities of impersonal love, tolerance, and total objectivity.

You are more impressionable now and a dreamer of the impossible dream. Déjà vu or daydreaming will not be uncommon. A 9 will help you separate what is no longer necessary or meaningful and aid you in keeping what is important, so that you can succeed in making the seemingly impossible a reality.

Think of a 9 encounter as being like cleaning your closet or attic. During this time, others may start projects or plans and you'll be required to complete the finishing touches. In the clothes and papers of past experiences lie precious memories, like forgotten pieces of china found after being stored away for so long. Amid the waste, you stumble upon your lost treasures.

The process of elimination and taking stock of yourself and your possessions can be very misunderstood by those who transit this period, because it can affect all parts of your being as well as outside physical happenings. These divisions—which bring about compassion, selfless service, and compact, polished results in the end—may instead be taken to mean pain, suffering, or loss. For example, you could experience the separation of an endearing friendship. On the surface this seems heartbreaking, but look again. It simply means that the friend has left the path you were traveling to follow a different fork in the road, while you maintain the direction you've chosen.

In a 9 Pinnacle, whatever appears to be taken or broken is really an addition to your growth, for it will be replaced by something or someone more suited to your needs. Any losses or delays experienced mean a preparation for the beginning of something else.

Emotions play a very important role. Control but not suppression is the key, and maintaining a broad outlook is vital. It will require that you view the pictures of experiences as a whole story, not just look at them as parts. During this time you will expand your field of endeavor either through research, study, school, teaching your knowledge to others, or being involved in philanthropic and humanitarian pursuits.

Number 9 is another one of the "limelight" numbers that can encompass a larger viewing audience. You will be involved amid and in front of groups of people through activity and/or entertainment. Books or movies on science fiction, romance, or mystery spark more of an interest now. Group get-togethers, writing projects, meetings, seminars, etc., all play a part during this period.

You will want to travel more. At least one of your vacations may include a long-distance trip. People from the past as well as individuals with diverse backgrounds make their entrance, some bearing gifts of expanded awareness. It's a time of gaining worldly experiences, as this transit provides tastes of a wide range.

A 9 contains a little bit of every other number's experiences in it. It also suggests that while you strive to extend your boundaries, you don't become a jack-of-all-trades and a master of none. You'll need to finish what you start, taking each situation, problem, project, or goal to its designated completion before you begin another venture.

It's a time of growth and a very dramatic time. You can be like a cedar chest full of valuable memorabilia and treasured rewards, collected and shared, by the time you leave this transit's threshold.

10

Challenges

△ Just as the Pinnacles of Life offer opportunities, the Challenges of Life present us with knowledge regarding a major area of our personality needing reinforcement. Although the Challenges can be similar to the missing numbers within the name, for they both refer to weakness and to the need to strengthen traits, the Challenges may not be as easily or obviously recognized. The missing numbers indicate mini-lessons; *the Challenges represent tests.*

The Challenges of Life simply mean an additional reminder of what needs work and regulation in order to keep things in perspective. Like a fallen tree that blocks the path in a road, the Challenges represent obstructions that could be encountered regularly by not using the qualities of that number properly, causing an impasse toward success. By jumping the log and overcoming the challenge, you can proceed along the road of life, uninterrupted and free of impediment.

There are four Challenges of Life, which are found from the birth date; however, the most important one is called the MAJOR CHALLENGE and remains with us throughout our days. The other three Challenges enter in for periods of time and are looked at in conjunction with the Major Challenge.

Before finding the Challenges represented by your birth date, a) *remember to reduce the compound numbers to single digits first* and b) *subtract the smaller number from the larger*

Begin calculating as follows:

1. Subtract the month and the day of birth. This is the first Minor Challenge and affects the life from birth to approximately twenty-eight years of age, but is especially active during the first Pinnacle of Life.
2. Subtract the day and the year of birth. This is considered the second Minor Challenge of Life and is in effect from approximately twenty-eight years of age to fifty-six years, but is most active during the transit of the second Pinnacle of Life.
3. Subtract the first Minor Challenge and the second Minor Challenge. This is called the third and MAJOR CHALLENGE of Life. *It is in effect from birth to the end of our days*, highly active during the transit of the third Pinnacle of Life. *This challenge is looked at in conjunction with the rest of the Challenges.*
4. Subtract the year and the month of birth. This is the fourth Minor Challenge and governs from the age of approximately fifty-six years through the rest of life and is particularly active during the fourth Pinnacle of Life; so its effects can be felt to a degree prior to age fifty-six.

Note: Remember to subtract the smaller number from the larger in the above directions.

The most important Challenge to scrutinize is the MAJOR CHALLENGE, for its effects are felt heavily on a consistent basis.

Let's take the same example as in the chapter on Pinnacles. The birth date that follows, once again, is that of the late John Lennon.

October 9 1940
10/1   9 14/5 = (15) 6 Birthpath

CHALLENGES

1st/Minor Challenge 8   4 2nd/Minor Challenge
           4 3rd/MAJOR Challenge
           4 4th/Minor Challenge

Everything flows in cycles, particularly in the timing of events and forecasting. One cannot say, for example, on January 1 of a particular year, right at that moment, one of your challenges will begin operation in full power. On occasion, there can be an overlap of Challenges as one eases out of the age period and the beginning of the next Challenge moves in. Let's use a hypothetical example to explain.

PINNACLES

      7   53 to end of life
      6   44 to 53
0 to 35   9   6   35 to 44
    May 4 1946
     5   4 20/2 = 11/2 BIRTHPATH

CHALLENGES

1st/Minor Challenge 1   2 2nd/Minor Challenge
           1 3rd/Major Challenge
           3 4th/Minor Challenge

Ordinarily, the first Minor Challenge ends its transit at approximately twenty-eight years of age and is especially active during the first Pinnacle of Life. In the above case, while the 1 as a first Minor Challenge eases out of its phase, the second Minor Challenge slowly moves in after twenty-eight years of age and can affect the first Pinnacle as well as the second Pinnacle of Life.

131

There are two Challenges in operation at once while focusing on the Major Challenge. The person in the chart above (in an attempt to bring about success between ages twenty-eight and thirty-five, while still in the first Pinnacle) must understand that through his broad experiences and the desire to expand his territory (9 Pinnacle), particular attention must be paid to how impulsively or forcefully he pushes (1 first Minor and 1 Major Challenge) to the top. He must practice self-reliance and originality, not forgetting the qualities of cooperation and tact (2 second Minor Challenge) along the way. In his case, the number 1 is intensified because it is found on both a Minor and Major Challenge position.

The Minor Challenges can interweave with one another, but *the Major Challenge affects us the most, for it shines over all four Pinnacles of Life and is most strongly felt during the third Pinnacle.*

Remember to scrutinize the Challenges along with the rest of the numbers you've been introduced to so far. For example, if your Major Challenge matches your Birthpath number, it indicates you challenge your very nature to succeed. Your inner talents will be tapped, yet you may be afraid to bring them out.

As another example, let's say your Major Challenge matches the total of your name. This indicates that along your field of endeavor and in your daily routines, you will be challenged in the outward expression of personality to maintain balance in those qualities.

From my professional experience, I've found that this position only tests your ability (unless that same number is missing within the letters, then it will teach and test) and does just what that number says, challenges you to a duel. In a sense, it is squaring off and asks, "Can you or can't you? And prove it." Success is never really handed to us on a silver platter. We have to work for what we want. The Challenges show you the little consistent ways in which to proceed and for what length of time.

Although each individual varies, the most commonly found Major Challenges are 1, 2, and 3. The next in succession are 4 and 5. Numbers 6, 7, and 8 are less frequently found and are outstanding challenges but capable of great reward for the effort expended. Number 9 will not be found in a Challenge position. As a prime digit, 9 is the highest number, and all others are subtracted from it. A 0 (zero) Challenge can be seen in some charts and is not as uncommon as some might think in this position.

The explanations below will pertain more specifically to the Major Challenge; however, those descriptions can also be applied to the other three Challenges during their period of operation.

Number One Challenge

During its time of operation, you will be nudged in the direction of leadership. It cautions you to balance your ego with your accomplishments. Are you afraid of taking the bull by the horns? If that's the case, you will be forced to anyway. Are you too headstrong and pushy? If this is your way of getting results, then the 1 Challenge will ask you to take a step or two back.

The key is balance between leadership and cooperation. It asks you to stand on your own two feet, give opinions, initiate plans when necessary, and take a chance on self-reliance and independence. It cautions you not to be caught up in the bossy, selfish, quick climb to the top.

Number Two Challenge

This Challenge may lead you to believe you don't have enough confidence or ability to undertake important projects. Remember, this is a test! The only person who doesn't think you can do it is you, no one else!

It warns you not to vacillate, play the martyr, or be overly sensitive to criticism but rather to effectively persuade and influence through gentle and diplomatic gestures. Believe that you can do what you feel you can.

It asks you not to be a doormat for someone else's whims but does request that you understand both personal and business relationships and know how to walk a mile in another person's shoes. It asks you to look at both sides of an issue before making judgments.

Number Three Challenge

You are entreated to believe in your own worth. There is a difference between lack of confidence and lack of self-worth. You can be your own worst enemy in that department. The 3 will engage you in a duel of balance between optimistic and pessimistic attitudes. You are to understand that in every gray cloud there is a silver lining, and sunnier days will always follow storms.

It cautions you not to talk too much, engage in gossip, or brag about yourself and your accomplishments to the point of overexaggeration. At the same time, it will encourage your sense of self-expression and creativity to come forth so that others may benefit. This Challenge will ask you to bring out your fine imagination and colorful gestures, putting them to good use by making others happy too. (P.S. Stop worrying so much. You're great at telling others how to have a worry-free life, but you don't always practice what you preach. No one sees what you put yourself through inwardly. You veil your fears in front of the public.)

Number Four Challenge

You can work hard and play hard. This Challenge asks you not to overdo, yet warns you not to be lazy either. You will need to keep your foundations firm through common sense, not stubbornness.

A 4 Challenge tests for weaknesses in laying foundations. How logical have you been and how much preplanning have you done beforehand? Is your base solid or spongy? It asks you to take things one step at a time and not to get caught up in restrictions that you've created through paperwork, promises, and projects taken on.

You can be an outward worrier by expressing frustrations you might feel, namely anxieties and anticipations of whether or not things will go right. This number challenges you to maintain your sense of integrity, loyalty, and stability and urges logical planning of goals and finances to ensure success.

Number Five Challenge

Either you like to mix and mingle with the public or you detest large gatherings. Number 5 represents freedom in every sense of the word. It would benefit you to mix with the public through your job or personal life. Through experiences, you will gain the knowledge of the proper use of personal freedom. It cautions you not to abuse its privileges by burning the candle at both ends or having too many irons in the fire at once.

Curiosity will spark questions and a quest to find out what's going on. Again, this feeling needs to be balanced, so that it's not misinterpreted as being nosy. Curiosity, however, will also ignite you to employ the proper manipulation of your mental and physical desires to gain the knowledge you seek.

Number Six Challenge

This is the Challenge of responsibility, adjustment, and acceptance. It adds a footnote of importance in the service given to others. Are you taken advantage of or do you actually expect too much in return? Balance between loving and letting go will be one of the tests.

The 6 in this position challenges your attitude toward responsibility. Serving with a smile is important, and so is understanding that lending a helping hand, whether at home or on the job, will be an invaluable gesture.

It warns you not to be possessive or to place too many expectations on others. It aids you in enhancing your ideas and maintaining them, as well as providing you with the ability to be a good listener and a caring individual.

Number Seven Challenge

This number tests the subjects of analyzation and intuition. You will be challenged to prove or look deeper into life's experiences; it requires more than just a scratching of the surface. Once you've approached the situation technically, analytically, and with much thought, then listen to your intuition, that catalytic moment (or gut instinct), and pay attention to it. The more you heed intuition's call, the more aware and sure you will become of the right answers it gives. How much do you rationalize or how often do you internalize? Herein lies a balancing between intellect and intuition.

What is reality and what is illusion? How well do you know the difference between the two? What is the difference between being alone rather than lonely? These and other questions will come up through observation or experience, testing you in the ability to understand and use the knowledge attained.

Number Eight Challenge

This is the challenge of values, organization, and spiritual and material aspects. It requires that you make the proper judgments through keen perception and efficient planning. It will test your ability to repeat efforts to ensure the best results. The 8 examines the handling of your money so that you learn not to overspend or penny-pinch, but to place the proper amount in the appropriate investments.

This Challenge symbolizes the keeping of material and spiritual matters in perspective by maintaining the proper ethics of everything you do. It tests your attitudes toward being happy in accomplishments as well as with monetary reward. This number challenges your overall sense of power and control, and urges you not to abuse the talent of delegation and the enormous drive you have to get to the top of the ladder.

Zero Challenge

What do you think of when you see a 0 (zero)? Is it a circle, a dial of some sort, a dot? The 0 is a rounded form connecting itself together with no openings. It represents the all or the nothing.

As a Challenge number, the 0 means you have a choice. You can either be challenged by all the numbers on different occasions or not be challenged at all. If you delude yourself into thinking you're perfect with the 0 in this position, you may find more challenges than you can handle. If you inwardly suspect all is not smooth in the makeup of your personality, then you have the option of deciding what attributes you need to work on and strengthen. Choosing in this manner can be a test in itself, a test of which is the right quality to pick.

The 0 means you have two options: taking the easy route by hitching a ride on someone else's coattails or doing it in your own way. The road may be bumpy and prove to be a longer route, but the destination and reward will be yours to claim, reached by you alone.

11

Your Very Own Individual Retirement Account

▲ In learning the basics of who you are from what you've read so far, there is one final number at which to look. *It is found by adding the Birthpath number to the total of the birth name and is called the RE-ALITY NUMBER.* Here's an example:

```
J A N E   M A R I E   S M I T H
1 1 5 5   4 1 9 9 5   1 4 9 2 8  = 64/10/1
                                       NAME
```

```
January 12 1952
    1    3 17/8  =  21/3 BIRTHPATH
```

1 NAME + 3 BIRTHPATH = 4 REALITY NUMBER

This number explains the sum total of the experiences of life and urges you to follow its qualities on a regulated basis, so that you can build up your account of security and long-lasting success for later days. This number represents your essence and can help you reach ultimate attainment, so that you will be assured of a happy and fulfilling time during the harvest days of living.

The Reality number carries a very subtle influence, which is almost unrecognizable during the teens through the mid-thirties, but can be perceived by children before they're influenced by outside activities, personal aims, and the requirements of the name total. The influences of this number will be most strongly felt sometime during the early and mid-fifties.

By looking at this number and its qualities, you may not believe it to feel or be like you, or you may not be familiar with the attributes because of lack of use. Begin, however, incorporating those characteristics a little at a time in your everyday routines, like a daily to-do list. By doing so, it will be like adding more money into your retirement account of security, collecting interest all the way.

In addition, this number can be considered one of your lucky numbers as well. I can't guarantee that you'll win at the races or bingo, but using this number and/ or your Birthpath digit might prove to be somewhat beneficial when playing games of chance.

Below are short, general descriptions of the Reality Number.

Number One Reality

Life will present many opportunities for you to use leadership and individuality. You will claim the title of "original" during later days of life and pioneer efforts for others. Don't be afraid to stand on your own two feet, no matter what age. Plan carefully but don't hesitate—move ahead. Any tendencies toward bossiness or being headstrong will cause problems with those whom you encounter. The 1 can represent a quick rise to the top, but it can also indicate a quick fall by not employing the proper attitudes and methods of authority and self-reliance.

Number Two Reality

Life urges you to practice tact and diplomacy to ensure the best it has to offer for later days. During the harvest years, more dealings with women and sensitive individuals will not be uncommon. Bringing opposing forces together into harmony will be a special talent you'll possess. Sensitive and feeling, you will gain knowledge either through religion or philosophy and manifest a gentle and somewhat humble quality. Lack of objectivity, inattention to detail, or vacillation will cause separations and problems connected with goals, plans, and people.

Number Three Reality

If you haven't felt creative or too imaginative during the first half of life, you will now. The 3 offers the chance to develop your colorful and gifted expression whichever way you choose. This can be an excellent time of life, offering popularity, love, romance, and very valued friends. You'll feel happier and more content if you begin practicing the qualities of optimism and find creative ways in which to express yourself. This number does caution you not to scatter your energies and to finish whatever you decide to start. Pessimistic or boastful tendencies will hamper and possibly destroy the joy that can surround you during the later days.

Number Four Reality

Making some of your dreams come true before now may have been difficult, for you may have done your share, but others may have gained the benefits. During the later days you will have the chance to cash in on your own accomplishments. You will have the discipline, strength, and endurance to implement your dreams into reality. Yes, you still have work to do. It suggests that an orderly system and practical application will be the means by which you gain the security you seek. Too much stubbornness or many fixed attitudes, as well as overworry either before or during the later days, will crack the structure of solidarity. Common sense, integrity, and stability build a life of happiness and peace of mind during your harvest days.

Number Five Reality

This number represents progress during the harvest years and can offer the freedom you seek. By implementing the art of communication and salesmanship, coupled with flexibility, you are promised an active, changing life-style. Restrictions or that caged feeling that may have been experienced prior to your later days will be lifted. You can soar like a bird, traveling to different parts of the land. You will not live your days in quiet solitude; work with the public will be enhanced. Doing too many things at once, either before or during this time, will spoil this marvelous period. Rather, seek out and experience life through one or two fields of endeavor and carry them to completion.

Number Six Reality

The home, hearth, and a comfortable luxurious way of living can be promised, full of family and friends if you practice the qualities of adjustment, service, and acceptance. Possessiveness or an argumentative nature will find you very much alone and laden with burdens instead of rewards. When you think of others and lend a helping hand as objectively as possible, this period will offer tremendous respect, financial support, and love.

Number Seven Reality

You can be offered a quiet and peaceful existence. By following the dictates of analyzation and intuition, 7 presents you with the opportunity to advance through technical trades, writing, or research in any area you choose. During your late forties and fifties, you may decide to secure a piece of property in the country or to reside in a place that offers the serenity of open spaces or water, away from the hustle and bustle. This time of life sparks resolution of your faith in a higher force, either through religion, metaphysics, or philosophical interests. You may wish to remain behind the scenes rather than in the limelight. If you have specialized and sought answers to your questions previously, then others will now seek out your wisdom with reverence and appreciation. Strong opinions or lack of introspection on life's meaning will find you lonely and confused.

Number Eight Reality

This is a dynamic time for you, full of responsibility and executive charge. Material matters as well as spiritual and philosophical investigations enhance the life and bring about a well-rounded and balanced way of living during later days. Overexerting your power, control, and influence to the detriment of others will find you having to dismount from the platform of leadership to pick up the broken pieces and start again. By maintaining keen perception, good judgment, and a zealous attitude toward the growth of everyone concerned, you are promised recognition and a very secure position in life.

Number Nine Reality

The humanitarian way you express yourself, impersonal love, and a broad outlook will umbrella the esteem you can enjoy during your later days. Philanthropy, drama, literature, the arts, etc., all give you the chance to attain prosperity and recognition. Yours is the way of service to the people. Courting self-love, personal gain, emotional outbursts, and expressions of subjective views will impede progress in drastic ways, causing losses or long-term delays in the very goals, friendships, and love you seek. Compassion, understanding of the whole picture, and a gregarious attitude full of wisdom and the desire to share it brings the best life has to offer during the retirement years.

Number Eleven Reality

The later days can be a time of revelation, inspiration, and gifted talent. You may invent, motivate, or energetically captivate your audience with the talent you possess. It can be an electric happening. You may be pushed into the limelight through entertainment, the arts, commercial enterprises, or education. Like the Statue of Liberty, who holds her torch high for all to see, you can be recognized as a landmark of inspired ideals. Just like the number 2, you will need to guard against indecision or flighty tendencies and at the same time, refrain from oversensitivity. By practicing the qualities of arbitration and consideration, zealously shining your guiding light, you can be rewarded with fame and fortune, as well as the satisfaction of inner contentment.

Number Twenty-Two Reality

You're being pushed into thinking and doing better things. The pursuit and realization of larger plans can be possible. You can be working smarter and not harder during the later days. Instead of building sand castles on the beach, you can create pyramids that are built in the desert. Don't think small, and try not to become deluged with too many restricting plans or projects that limit your scope. During the harvest days, you can be like the Master Builder, who oversees the plans and actions of others, as you scan, project, and implement the next steps toward accomplishment and fulfillment—*if* you don't narrow your steps beforehand. Go for it!

Number Thirty-Three Reality

Another one of the Master Numbers, 33 places you in situations where you can teach others through example during your later days of life. As you reach your fifties, others begin more and more to look up to you and your ideals. Bursting with energy and uplifted with enthusiasm, you can be involved in community, health services, or government institutions, not to mention educational arenas. You can have a healing effect on others through your sensitive and calm inner disposition. You're promised the love and harmony you desire, as well as the recognition received from the service you give. Chaotic actions, explosive arguments, or embittered, cynical jealousies will completely dismember your fortress of tranquility, financial security, and loving companionship. Piece by piece it will break down, leaving you bare and cold, forcing you to switch your attitude back, to balance and begin again. The responsibilities of this number are great during later days, but so too is the complete satisfaction and reward promised you.

12

The Connection Between Numerology and Astrology

O Numerology, quite simply, is the study of the science of numbers. The link to this modern-day science, as we know it, has been credited to Pythagoras. He believed that everything related to numbers, including physical traits and tendencies. In other words, numbers have a language in addition to being used for keeping time and measuring quantities. He believed that the "principles that govern the numbers are the principles of real existence."

To Pythagoras, numbers were representative of sounds, patterns, and rhythms. He discovered the mathematical relationship between the various tones of the diatonic scale. There was created a syncopated and melodic harmony among numbers, a type of music relating ourselves and the universe as a whole.

In the field of astrology, planets are described by traits and tendencies (Mars represents action, Mercury represents the mind, etc.). These descriptions can also be represented by numbers that symbolize their meaning. It has been suggested that Pythagoras began to associate or link numerals with the planets of the solar system. However, because some of the teachings of Pythagoras were lost and because not all of the planets we know today were discovered in the time before Christ, there is occasional controversy among astrologers and numerologists as to which numbers represent which planets. However, there is no dispute concerning the close link numerology and astrology have as brother and sister sciences.

One of the connecting cords between the two sciences is in this planet/number fellowship. I have compiled a list of such associations below. These are "seeds" that have been planted for you to think about. As we gain more knowledge, retrieve what has been lost, and add to what we discover in the future, I'm sure there will be others like myself who can give even more insight into this close relationship between numbers and planets.

There are many layers to an onion, for example, and each one can be peeled back and examined. So it should be understood that in numerology, just as in astrology, you can have more than one layer of interpretation, depending upon the level of operation through the individual.

The following list of number/planet associations will have more than one planet assignment in some cases, with those that have a more subtle influence marked in parentheses. For now, based on my ten years of experience with numerology as well as its relation to planetary aspects, what is explained here is the research data I've collected.

NUMBER	PLANETS
1	Mars/Sun
2	Moon (Venus)
3	Jupiter (Mercury)
4	Earth (Saturn)
5	Mercury/Uranus
6	Venus/Saturn (Mercury)
7	Neptune/Uranus (Vulcan*)
8	Saturn/Mars (Pluto)

9	Jupiter/Mars/Uranus
	(Neptune has a slight influence)
11/2	Uranus/Moon (Venus)
22/4	Pluto/Earth (Saturn)
33/6	Chiron/upper octave Venus/?*
	*needs more research

As you can see, the number 33/6 has a question mark. In my estimation, there is at least one more planet that can be associated with this number. It is Neptune, planet of high spirituality, illusion, and service, many times, to mankind. At its ultimate, this numeral represents the Master Teacher. When it is expressed on the highest level, the 33/6 can be magnetic, learning to express unconditional love and service as it sheds its illuminating and strong, yet calming influences over the masses. Each planet describing this number in an attempt to explain its meaning seems only to touch the surface of its humanitarian meaning.

In my professional opinion, astronomers and astrologers have and will be discovering even more in the future. As research continues into the understanding of number/planet associations, we may discover additional insight.

Perhaps in your quest for the truth, you will take what is presented here and plant the seeds of more knowledge through your own investigation. I hope you do.

Closing Remarks

I hope this book has proven enjoyable and can aid you in the discovery of who you are. It has been a pleasure for me to share this knowledge with you. Being a numerologist, I am completely fascinated with the accuracy and in-depth perception of numerology and am glad Pythagoras decided to research and expand his knowledge of numbers in relation to psychological traits.

When I first began to understand what numbers meant beyond the spectrum of keeping time and measuring quantities, I was indeed skeptical. Priding myself as having logical and analytical capabilities, I thought to myself, "How can numbers tell us anything other than quantitative statements?" That is how I became interested in this science. It challenged me to prove its accuracy as a language, and I did just that! Even today, I still chuckle and shake my head at how precise this science really is. Believe me, most of my clients, both locally and nationally, react the same way. It works! That's all there is to it.

There is much more to knowing and charting numerology than is contained in these pages. This book has given you the basics—and hopefully whetted your appetite by introducing this subject to you. There are other things you can learn from it: finding your personal year, which is a more specific means of forecasting, calculating the subpaths, which are like rest stops along the road of the Birthpath qualities, and/or obtaining the Planes of Expression, which can aid in picking apart the personality. There is so much more to learn after absorbing what has been presented to you so far.

There are other books that are excellent reading material on this subject and can increase your awareness even beyond the point I have taken you. I hope you reach out and expand upon the basics. In the meantime, I'm working on another book to follow this one. Until then, have fun exploring and applying what you've read.

> *If a man does not keep pace*
> *with his companions,*
> *perhaps it is because*
> *he hears a different drummer.*
> *Let him step*
> *to the music which he hears,*
> *however measured or far away.*

> —HENRY DAVID THOREAU

Vowel Totals _____

			First Name		19

Vowel Numbers		5		9	5									
N A M E (birth cert.)	L	E	S	L	I	E								
Consonant Numbers	3		1	3										

					7	
Consonant Totals _____						

```
                        7
Pinnacles  →           / \              ← 47 to end of
+ add                 / 9 \             ← 38 to 47 yrs
                     / \ / \
  36-Birthpath      7   X   2           ← 29 to 38 yrs
Ages: to 29 yrs →  /         \
```

Birthday →

6	28	1954
Month	Day	Year

6	1	¹⁹/10/1	=	8
				Birthpath

```
Challenges  →        \   5   0   /
- subtract            \   \ /   /
                       \   5   /
                        \     /
                           5
```

● **PRESENT NAME**

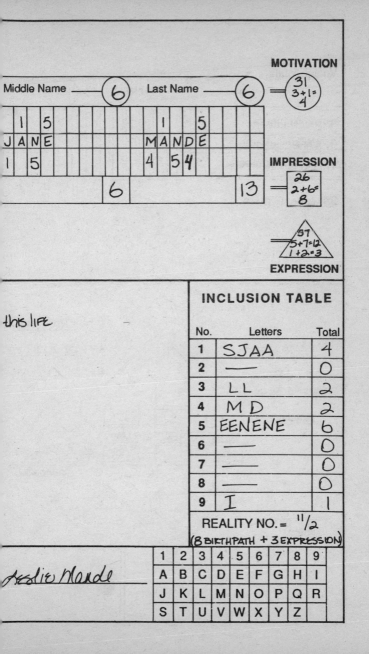

MOTIVATION

Middle Name —— (6)   Last Name —— (6)   = $\dfrac{\begin{array}{c}31\\3+1=\\4\end{array}}{}$

	1	5							1		5			
J	A	N	E					M	A	N	D	E		
1		5						4		5	4			

6   13

IMPRESSION

= $\dfrac{\begin{array}{c}26\\2+6=\\8\end{array}}{}$

$\dfrac{\begin{array}{c}57\\5+7=12\\1+2=3\end{array}}{}$

EXPRESSION

this life

INCLUSION TABLE

No.	Letters	Total
1	SJAA	4
2	—	0
3	LL	2
4	MD	2
5	EENENE	6
6	—	0
7	—	0
8	—	0
9	I	1

REALITY NO. = $^{11}/_2$

(8 BIRTHPATH + 3 EXPRESSION)

Leslie Mande

1	2	3	4	5	6	7	8	9	
A	B	C	D	E	F	G	H	I	
J	K	L	M	N	O	P	Q	R	
S	T	U	V	W	X	Y	Z		

Vowel Totals _____

First Name _____ ◯

Vowel Numbers																	
N A M E (birth cert.)																	
Consonant Numbers																	

Consonant Totals _____

Pinnacles →
+ add

36-Birthpath

Ages: _____ →

Birthday →

Month		Day		Year	

= _____

Birthpath

Challenges →
- subtract

● **PRESENT NAME**

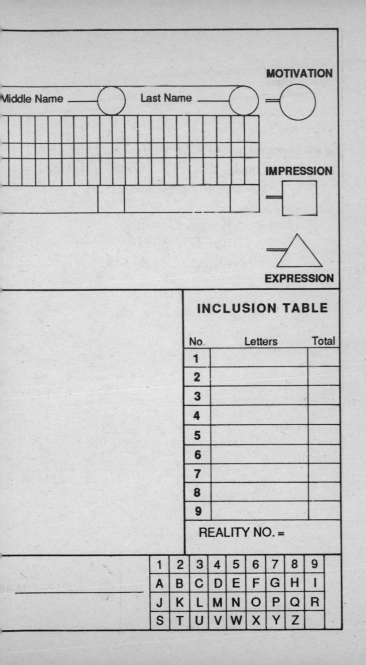

MOTIVATION

Middle Name ———○ Last Name ———○ ═○

IMPRESSION

═□

EXPRESSION

△

INCLUSION TABLE

No.	Letters	Total
1		
2		
3		
4		
5		
6		
7		
8		
9		

REALITY NO. =

1	2	3	4	5	6	7	8	9
A	B	C	D	E	F	G	H	I
J	K	L	M	N	O	P	Q	R
S	T	U	V	W	X	Y	Z	

Karen David would be happy to hear from the readers of *I'VE GOT YOUR NUMBER*. Please write to her at:

Karen David
P.O. Box 39216
Cleveland, OH 44139